FAMILY PREPAREDNESS
FOR THE
NEW MILLENNIUM

FAMILY PREPAREDNESS
FOR THE
NEW MILLENNIUM

DAVID BROWNE

iUniverse LLC
Bloomington

FAMILY PREPAREDNESS FOR THE NEW MILLENNIUM

iUniverse books may be ordered through booksellers or by contacting:

iUniverse LLC
1663 Liberty Drive
Bloomington, IN 47403
www.iuniverse.com
1-800-Authors (1-800-288-4677)

ISBN: 978-1-4917-0452-3 (sc)
ISBN: 978-1-4917-0454-7 (hc)
ISBN: 978-1-4917-0453-0 (ebk)

Library of Congress Control Number: 2013915615

Printed in the United States of America

iUniverse rev. date: 08/24/2013

Chapter 1

This is the future!

What do you think will happen in the near future?
Let's take a look at what has happened first.

1. 2008 financial crisis (collapse/bailout phase): September/October 2008 What the Fed did:

    - On Sept. 8, 2008, the U.S. Treasury seized control of mortgage giants Fannie Mae and Freddie Mac and pledged a $200 billion cash injection to help the companies cope with mortgage default losses.
    - About a week later the government bailed out American International Group Inc., or AIG, with $85 billion.
    - The Fed refused to save Lehman Brothers and the company was forced to file for bankruptcy. Some of the largest financial institutions were on the verge of collapse as the mortgage market melted down. As the crisis hit the global market, the credit freeze spread.
    - The Treasury and the Federal Reserve began working on a $700 billion bailout plan.
    - President George W. Bush signed the bailout plan into law Oct. 3.

- Weeks later, on Oct. 29, the Fed cut the key interest rate to 1 percent. Read more: http://www.bankrate. com/finance/federal-reserve/financial-crisis-timeline. aspx#ixzz2ZWDuegVG

2. The all items index increased 1.8 percent over the last 12 months, an increase from last month's 1.4 percent figure. The index for all items less food and energy has risen 1.6 percent over the last year, the smallest 12-month change since June 2011. The energy index has risen 3.2 percent over the span, and the food index has increased 1.4 percent.

New release, July 16th, 2013; Bureau of Labor Statistics.

3. Misery Index (8.96) equals Unemployment rate (7.6) plus Inflation rate (1.36). The misery index was initiated by economist Arthur Okun, an adviser to President Lyndon Johnson in the 1960's. It is simply the unemployment rate added to the inflation rate. It is assumed that both a higher rate of unemployment and a worsening of inflation create economic and social costs for a country. A combination of rising inflation and more people out of work implies a deterioration in economic performance and a rise in the misery index.

4. "The American dream is dead for the majority of America," financial guru Suze Orman told Forbes last year, speaking about her upcoming book "The Money Class"

5. Surveys show meager growth in average wages of 1.7 percent in the past year, while surges in gasoline and food prices have pushed the inflation rate to more than 2 percent. Growth in other sources of income such as rents, interest and Social Security has been weak or nonexistent. The result-typical workers are no

longer able to keep up with the rising cost of living. <u>Washington Times, Patrice Hill, April 5, 2011.</u> If it was that bad back then it is a lot worse now!

6. Consumer Confidence is at an all time low, just ask yourself that question.

7. The number of Americans receiving food stamps as reported by the United States Department of Agriculture: As of the latest data released on July 5, 2013, the total is 47.5 million, which is more than the entire populations of many large nations. It is almost inconceivable that the largest economy on earth could have so many people dependent on the government food handout.

8. As the economy crumbles, we are also witnessing the fabric of society begining to come apart. The recent flash of gang crimes that we are starting to see all over America is just one example of this. When laundry detergents and food are becoming a target of burglary, things are not looking good for the near future. Gangs are living in bank reposessed homes that are left vacant.

9. Some desperate Americans are already stealing anything that they can get their hands on. For example, according to the American Kennel Club, dog thefts are up 32 percent the last year. People need to eat?

10. The recent flash mob crimes that we are starting to see all over America, are yet another example of this.

11. The United States national debt is like a giant boulder that our economy must constantly carry around on its back, and it is growing by billions of dollars every single day. At

the time of writing, the debt of the federal government is $14,592,242,215,641.90. It has gone up by nearly 4 trillion dollars since Barack Obama took office. S&P has already stripped the United States of its AAA credit rating, and more downgrades are certain to come if the United States does not get its collective financial act together.

12. Tensions between the United States and China are rising again. A new opinion piece on chinadaily.com is calling for the Chinese government to use its holdings of United States debt as a "financial weapon" against the United States if the United States follows through with a plan to sell more arms to Taiwan. The United States and China are the two biggest economies in the world, so any trouble between them would mean economic trouble for the rest of the globe as well.

13. Courtesy of Economic Policy Journal we now know that the majority of American States are currently insolvent, and that the US Treasury has been conducting a shadow bailout of at least 32 US states. Over 60% of Americans receiving state unemployment benefits are getting these directly from the US government, as 32 states have now borrowed $37.8 billion from Uncle Sam to fund unemployment insurance.

14. ART. 3: Manifesto of United Future World Currency states: "It is therefore our wish to bring to life the project for a common currency, which has been given the provisional names, 'Eurodollar/Dollaeur' (initially), 'United Money', then 'United Future World Currency'. It would symbolize not only the economic, but also the human, social, political, and spiritual bonds between the Nations of different Continents that hold similar ideals."

15. The European sovereign debt crisis continues to deepen. Countries like Portugal, Italy and Greece are on the verge of an economic abyss. All of the financial problems in Europe are beginning to affect the core European nations. For example, German industrial production declined by 1.1% in June 2011 alone. There are all kinds of signs that the economy of Europe is slowing down and is heading for a protracted recession. French President Nicolas Sarkozy and German Chancellor Angela Merkel are proposing that a new economic government for Europe be established to oversee the current crisis, but nothing that the Europeans have attempted thus far has alleviated any problems.

16. The United States, Canada and Mexico are to merge into a single new entity named the North American Union. Its government, articles and constitution and MONEY will be merged. Take a look at the new coin.

17. The Federal Reserve is so desperate to bring some sort of stability to financial markets that it has stated that it will likely keep interest rates near zero all the way until mid-2013. The Federal Reserve is operating in panic mode almost constantly now and they are almost out of ammunition. So what is going to happen when the real trouble starts?

18. Central banks around the world certainly seem to be preparing for something. According to the <u>World Gold Council</u>, central banks around the globe purchased more gold during the first half of 2011 than they did all of last year.

19. <u>NaturalNews. Com by Ethan Huff, staff writer. December 10, 2011</u>

Federal agents raid Mormon food storage facility, demand list of customers storing emergency food. Later a door-to-door questioning of Tennessee citizens about their stored food.

20. Chinese Troops Reportedly Amassing Near US-Mexico Border—video shows potential military base. <u>Beforeitsnews. com The Video was banned by FEMA. This book might be banned too.</u>

21. <u>mnn.com/earth March 7, 2011 by Bryan Nelson;</u> The magnetic north pole is currently shifting at a faster rate than at any time in human history—almost 40 miles a year—and some experts believe that it may be the beginning of a complete pole reversal.

22. <u>Mailonline.com, by Eddie Wrenn, 10 july 2012</u> NASA, The sun is a tempestuous mistress—and her outbursts are becoming more and more violent as the weeks go on. NASA's Solar Dynamics Observatory spotted the summer's first 'X' solar flare on Friday—a huge outburst from the sun right at the top of the scale.

23. <u>Policymic.com by George Ivanov</u> Isreal's war with Iran is Imminent: Gaza, Syria, and Egypt are to blame.

24. How many FEMA Concentration camps are there in the United States? 800 that we know of. <u>Nstarzone.com/camps</u>

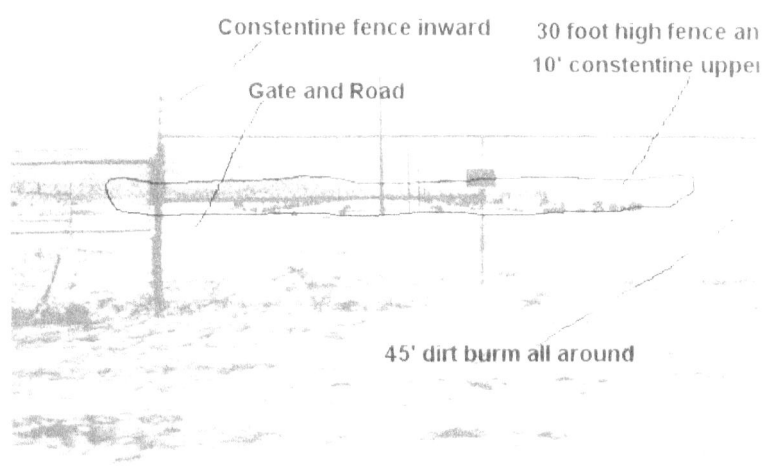

25. Aug 1995, Cedar City Airport, I personally watched two C-147 Army aircraft fly in and land, and two Army buses rolled up as some 40 Russians in uniform and two, two star Generals took a bus trip to all military bases and who knows what for a two week tour.

26. On February 3, 2012, a judge declared that the Food and Drug Administration had jurisdiction over all private property use with regard to Pennsylvania farmer Dan Allgyer's livestock. Selling raw milk, cheese, eggs and butter are now apparently prohibited activity. One might think that this blatant interference in free commerce and would be against the Commerce Clause, but apparently when it is outright banned by the Federal Government with no law specifically granting federal jurisdiction to do so, it is still acceptable. There is a word that accurately describes this type of governance: Tyranny.

27. The Center for Security Policy, suggests that an Electro-Magnetic Pulse (EMP) or CME could easily result in widespread inductance generated damage to our electrical distribution grid across the United States and beyond, and could potentially leave 90% of Americans dead within the first year. Question: Why? Answer: Because as a nation, we did not prepare for it. Many of the cold war era protections against EMP such as TEMPEST, are no longer in use due to the added costs.

28. Working-class whites are gloomy about future amid rising income gaps, racial shifts.

   AP*By Hope Yen, Associated Press | Associated Press*—July, 28, 2013 WASHINGTON (AP)—Four out of five U.S. adults struggle with joblessness, near-poverty or reliance on welfare for at least parts of their lives, a sign of deteriorating economic security and an elusive American dream.

   Survey data exclusive to The Associated Press points to an increasingly globalized U.S. economy, the widening gap between rich and poor and the loss of good-paying manufacturing jobs quoted as reasons for the trend.

   The findings come as President Barack Obama tries to renew his administration's emphasis on the economy, saying in recent speeches that his highest priority is to "rebuild ladders of opportunity" and reverse income inequality.

29. The United States Department of Homeland Security has awarded a contract for 450,000,000 rounds of .40 caliber

handgun ammunition. That is an incredibly excessive amount for practice ammunition. To put it another way, it is enough for one and a half bullets for every man, woman and child in the United States.

30. **And finally, the Mark of the Beast** that we have been waiting for is here. Obama Health Care Mandate Mar 2013 to be completed in 3 years by the Secretary of State. Read it for yourself. On page 1001, to be inserted in the left hand, a class II or a class III radio transmitter that will contain all your personal history, medical history and banking information.

    It will be mandatory on all food stamps, medical assistance, military, schools, unemployment recipients to begin with. Anyone who wants something from the government will be required to have this device implanted.

31. This, I believe, will bring on many of the riots as people demand food, medical help etc. I think it will begin in the bible belt first as those good spiritual people realize that this is the Mark of the Beast.

    I could go on for another 100 examples but I hope this will be enough for you to read "Family Preparedness for the New Millennium's.

    Now lets get started on how you can prepare for this anarchy.

Chapter 2

Neighborhood Emergency Training Team (NETT)

We went over the idea of the Electrical Grid going down and what to do in that case. Here are some other areas to plan for on your block and how to develop your NETT for further protection.

My first introduction to the concept of NETT was while I was stationed at Fort Ord, California during the Watts Riots. I had to pull extra guard duty during this week with an unloaded M14 rifle. While patrolling the streets I noticed that a couple of former marines (they were in uniforms) had barricaded the street leading to their homes with cars and whatever else they could find. The rioters walking down the main street went right on by their street. These people took matters into their own hands and provided for the security needs of their own families and neighborhood. The idea of neighborhood emergency teams was born.

I would like to point out plainly and clearly that this type of action is not vigilantism. Vigilantism is taking the law into your own hands in an environment where law and order exists in some form. When law and order breaks down, you have every right to protect yourself, your family and your property. Do not let anyone convince you otherwise.

Should you have an emergency or anarchy in your area, you will have to decide whether or not to stay and stand your ground or get out of Dodge. You will want to plan how you are going to shelter-in-place and protect your homes. What follows are a few ideas that I developed over the years. I will not plan it for you because someone might misinterpret that I support vigilantism. I wholeheartedly support family preparedness and security. If you have anarchy in the streets you have to do what you need to do to survive or better yet, disengage from the situation and leave the area for safety until the situation improves. The cost of a hotel or motel away from danger is money well spent. In fact, you really do not even need to spend money in hotels at all if you are prepared with camping gear or can stand sleeping in your vehicle until the dust settles. Obviously, if the situation is expected to be a protracted, long-term event, you may want to dig in and hunker down or get out of town. I will show you how in the next chapter.

In order to stay in your homes you must have food, water and security in appropriate quantity. How you keep that triad intact is up to you. One thing is certain; it will take prior planning. When the situation develops, it is too late to go shopping for needed supplies. You want to first think about what is most likely to happen in your particular area and then begin to make appropriate plans for those situations first. Keep in mind that part of this planning is to acquire all the necessary supplies and have a working knowledge of all your gear. Once that is done and in place, move to the next step, begin to think of a few contingencies and plan for those as well. Over time, you will have amassed enough supplies, gear, knowledge, practice and experience to withstand a myriad of emergencies, and that is our ultimate goal.

• Planning for Contingencies

Understand that you can neither plan for everything nor think of every eventuality. It is easy to go to the extreme and wind up spending loads of money on things meant to address ocurrences that are so remote they are negligible. For instance, it makes no sense to prepare for blizzards in Florida. Could snow fall in Florida? The answer is yes and it has, but it never sticks around long enough to cause a situation lasting more than a day. Try to limit your planning to the top four or five problems that are plausible in your area. Incorporate your neighbors into the planning as to create overlapping protection against those problems.

A few ideas to think about and plan for:

- Electrical Failure
- Water System Failure
- Natural Gas Failure
- Food Shortages
- Riots or Anarchy
- Martial Law
- Relocation

• Electrical Failure

First, let's look at our dependence on electricity. Take stock of everything in your home that is plugged into house current (a.k.a. 110 or 220 volts). If you have an electric range or oven, you need electricity to operate it. The lights in our homes are nearly exclusively electrically powered; I do not know of anyone who uses kerosene, candles or whale oil to light their homes anymore. If your home has no natural gas service, chances are good that your hot water and central heating are both electrically driven as well. If you are on well water, add your water pump to the list. We have not even mentioned anything about all the other conveniences such as lights, hair dryers, radios, televisions, computers, cable or satellite service, iPod, iPad, iPhone chargers; the list goes on and on. In many homes, the main form of energy used is electricity. What happens when it shuts off?

Your first concern when the power goes off, whether short or long term, is medical equipment. If you are on breathing machines or other devices requiring electricity, do not hesitate to send up the flag. Find some way to let someone know that you need help. Thankfully, most people in this country do not have to rely on these life-prolonging technologies.

The next concern on the list is the first concern on most people's list. What will you do with the food in the refrigerator or freezer? You will need to determine the likelihood of the return of electrical service. If the reason for the outage is a car crash down the street, chances are good that the power will be back on within a few hours. Anything longer than that, better plan on using up your refrigerated foods first. When I was a kid, this was a happy time because it was open season on all the ice cream. Vegetables and steaks will not leak all over the place, so they can be preserved at least over the next few hours. If you do not have some form of backup power, you should plan to use these things up first and fast.

I happened upon a great deal at the local warehouse store and picked up two 2000-watt voltage inverters. An inverter takes 12 volts direct current (DC) and inverts it to 110 volts alternating current (AC). You can hook these up to your car's battery terminals and provide power to your refrigerator or freezer for a few hours at a time throughout the day. This will keep the appliances working enough to prevent spoilage. Have the engine running to handle the load since these appliances will quickly deplete your vehicle's battery power. If your battery is dead and you cannot start your car, you might be left without power of any kind. Procedure planning will help avoid these problems.

Once you have safeguarded your foods, you can begin to use excess power for other purposes. Lighting at night is good not only for morale, but also to prolong your time available for work or other activities. If you have to budget to replace all your incandescent or compact fluorescent (CF) light bulbs with light emitting diode (LED) bulbs, begin doing so immediately. Not only will they save a surprising amount of money on your current electrical bills, but they also will cause far less taxing on your battery or other backup power systems; an extremely important consideration when operating on emergency systems. They are quite expensive, but they last much longer than traditional incandescent or CF bulbs in addition to being far less power hungry.

The best solution for a long term outage is to have a generator. As for capacity planning, keep in mind that you can live without air conditioning for a while because sweat will not cost you a lot of money. A larger generator will burn through your stored fuels faster than a smaller one. You do not want to lose hundreds of dollars' worth of refrigerated foods, especially if you have to depend upon those foods you have on-hand to sustain your family through an emergency. If air conditioning is a priority, then you will need to spend more money on a model that delivers in sufficient quantity and has the capacity to store the added fuel requirements.

Solar and wind power are alternatives to commercial power, however they are expensive and more suitable for small loads in rural areas. Chances are good that if you are in a rural area, you do not need to be overly concerned about rioting and anarchy. You will have different problems to attend to.

Conduct at least annual "plugs-out" testing of your alternative energy plan. Be sure you know how to connect your appliances to your power sources and operate them safely. Ensure that you have the proper amount of oil in your generator before starting it and every time you need to refill the fuel tank. It sounds like a no-brainer, but those are the little details that can come back around to bite you when you need it least.

> ***What-2-Do?:*** *Share this knowledge with your neighbors. The more independent they make themselves, the less dependent upon you they will be in an emergency. In a NETT setting, you may even have the ability to share power and refrigeration resources. By consolidating your resources, you can stretch your fuel, power, food and other resources farther than you all would be able to do independently.*

- Water System Failure

This is one situation that you will want to act quickly upon, especially if you are on a municipal water system. Water is essential to good health, and the more you have stored, the better off you will be. You really cannot have too much water stored up. To last one week, you will need at least 6 gallons per person; more if you value things such as cooking, bathing and laundering.

The first thing you want to do is shut off the main water valve feeding your home. This will trap many gallons of usable water in your pipes that can later be drained from a low point in your system. If you leave the main valve open and you turn on an upstairs water valve or flush an upstairs toilet, the water will drain out of the house due to lack of feed pressure. If you turn on a faucet and you hear air sucking in, turn it off immediately; your water service has gone kaput.

You can still obtain water from your hot water heater, but ensure that it is turned off at the circuit breaker or fuse panel. If it kicks on with no water in the tank, it can be damaged rather quickly. With the water that is trapped in your water pipes and your water heater, you should be able to have enough potable water to withstand emergencies of a few days. Anything longer than that, you will have to start seeking water from other sources.

Many cities no longer allow well drilling, but if your town allows it, consider a private well to supply the water you will need during long term outages, even if you stay on city water systems. It's never a bad thing to have more than one option! If you do have a well drilled upon your property, ensure that you have an independent electrical system to drive the pump or have a manual means to bring water up to the surface in appreciable quantities.

Another option you may have (if you live in an area that has appreciable rainfall) is you collect the rain water from your roofs. This water will require filtration and sterilization before it can be used safely as potable water, but it can yield hundreds of gallons from even a small roof in a short time. If you have gutters already installed on your eaves, you already have most of the necessary pieces in place. Route the fall into rain barrels instead of spilling onto the ground and you will have a significant and re-plenishable supply of water. Bear in mind that you cannot control the frequency of rainfall, so be sure to use this water judiciously.

> **What-2-Do?:** *Take stock of the things you have on-hand that can be used to produce or collect water. Instead of recycling or throwing away clear 2 liter soda*

bottles, fill them with water then store them in some unused space in your house or apartment and change the water out twice a year. These plastic soda bottles are transparent to UV sunlight, so they can be used as a solar sterilizer. Glass bottles block UV sunlight and will not kill any biological content in the water. You will still need to filter for metals, minerals and other chemical content, but this is a cheap and easy way to sterilize water.

- ## Natural Gas Failure

If you live in an earthquake prone area and there are problems with natural gas delivery, this can be a very bad thing. Fires can erupt at any point along the mains where there are breaks and gas is escaping. If you detect the pungent smell of gas in your home, get out fast and do not touch any light switches along the way. You do not want to provide the spark that sets off an explosion.

__What-2-Do?:__ If you store gas in LP tanks, keep them in good repair and fill them fairly frequently. If it takes you two months to burn through your fuel, have it topped off every three or four weeks. This will ensure that you have a fairly good supply of fuel should the logistical chain break down

- ## Food Shortages

This is one area where nobody should be unprepared. In the United States, food is relatively cheap and plentiful. You should have no less than a week's worth of calories for every person in your charge in your pantry at all times. Canned goods often have an expiration date, but this is not so much a date of usability as it is a date of peak freshness. They should still be safe for consumption unless the seal is obviously faulty.

The government recommends that you have a 72-Hour supply of food to get you through an emergency. Consider this; how long did it take for relief supplies to reach the victims of Hurricane Katrina? It was obviously more than 72 hours for a large number of them in both urban and rural areas. The 72-Hour packs as designed to keep you alive just long enough to be relocated to a government shelter where you can be cared for with all the compassion and tenderness of the FEMA. The point is that you absolutely need much more than this overly optimistic figure. Your goal should be more than a week's worth of food all the way up to total sustainable independence.

The military's Meals: Ready to Eat (MREs) are good for what they are designed for; combat. They have a constipating effect on your digestive system, and when you finally have no choice but to go to the bathroom, it will feel akin to childbirth! The bottom line is that they are designed to provide a lot of calories and allow a soldier to fight on for a few days without being slowed down by diarrhea. They are not suitable for long term use, but if you are traveling on foot, they can get you through some tough days.

If you are looking for a long-term, replenishable and sustainable food source, you will have to do some major planning, put in some diligent work and be able to plan far in advance. The upshot is that you will not be catastrophically affected by interruptions in the local supermarket's logistics. The downside is that the same hurricane that cut off supply to your supermarket can wipe out your garden. You will still want to have plenty of food in storage as well as on the vine.

Here is another point to consider; what if the event occurred while you were at work? What foods do you have stored at work to get you through a couple days, not just until the next break? Do you have some long-term stores in your car? If you find yourself lacking, consider keeping some camper's delights stored in your car such as water, vienna sausage, baked beans, canned soup, tea and sugar. These items will keep for a long time (ironically, the tea has the shortest shelf life) and can come in handy even if a large scale event does not take place. Happenings such as being stranded in a snowstorm or being lost and out of gas may occur. Do you have a locker at work? Consider storing some items there as well, and do not forget to include a can opener and utensils!

> ***What-2-Do?:*** *You may want to learn about aquaponics and build your own system. Not only do they provide for growing vegetables, but also fish that can be culled for meat. Specifically, Tilapia is a robust, compact and highly reproductive species to use in apuaponics.*

- Riots or Anarchy

This is where the danger from two-legged predators is at its' zenith. There is no more terrifying prospect that people can face than that of a lawless mob hell bent on killing people and taking their stuff. It is an extremely stressful time that can drive people to do things they would never think about under normal circumstances. As repugnant as taking another life is, it is at times necessary to protect innocent lives and to prevent further bloodshed. You must know your neighbors, strengths, weaknesses, who you can trust and not trust.

> ***What-2-Do?:*** *If you are faced with such a situation, you have to mentally detach your moral norms and think in mathematical terms. If taking one life can save ten, then you must make that decision and act on it instantly. God can forgive whatever and whoever he wants to. The person pointing a weapon at your family has had ample opportunity to get right with*

God. If you have the means to arrange the meeting, you need to have steel in your spine and do it to protect your family and anyone else under your charge. The old adage is true: it's better to be judged by twelve than carried by six.

• Martial Law

Under normal times, this is a country based on law; of governance by, for and of the people. That is not to say that government cannot turn on its' master and become like a tyrant, answerable only unto itself. It can, and thankfully, it rarely has in the past. One can point to Abraham Lincoln's suspension of habeus corpus or Franklin Roosevelt's highly illegal internment of American citizens (without cause other than their race) during WWII to provide two of the most notable examples.

Lincoln once remarked that the Constitution is not a suicide pact, and he was right. The Federal Government can take action in defense of our national security, which basically means the lives and freedoms of United States Citizens. It is a fine line between defense and deprivation of freedoms, and it is an issue that must not be taken lightly by either the Federal Government or the citizenry. Martial law can be declared to protect the lives of citizens in a disaster area or an area under military or terrorist attack. I cannot think of anything else that would justify the military's operation domestically.

The good news is this however; military personnel are generally keenly aware of their oath to protect and defend the Constitution of the United States against all enemies, foreign and domestic. They are highly averse to taking action against American citizens and they do not pledge allegiance to the President. They are under no obligation to follow illegal orders, and even lowly privates generally know it.

If Martial law is declared in your area, it will be your decision whether or not to comply. You are the boots-on-the-ground person and you will have to make the decision to go along or get going. If you begin to see your neighbors rounded up under suspect circumstances or nebulous reasons, it might be time to pull stakes and head for the hills (if you still can). If you cannot, then keep in mind that there are things not worth getting shot over. The military has night vision capabilities, so your plans to stroll away under the cover of darkness might not be the best avenue of retreat. You may have to get creative in your escape and evasion skills.

> **What-2-Do?:** *Never underestimate the power of bribery. If a couple packs of cigarettes can get you past a check point or get you some much needed food, then by all means, do so. Understand that under Martial law, you are not going to get far by taking on and going against those in charge. Do not get aggressive when they have guns and you don't. You're not going to win. You will have to use your brains rather than*

your brawn to get through hard times, and nothing I could tell you in this book can fully prepare you. You are the commander on the ground and will have to make the call as to how you and your family should act. It's time to man up.

- Relocation

If you wait until after a disaster, an attack or a riot starts, your chances of getting out of town are going to be reduced and it could be much more difficult and much more dangerous. The inner city will most likely be the most dangerous areas and thus should be avoided if at all possible. The name of this game is stealth, don't stand out, blend in and act like one of them. Don't get caught so you don't go here.

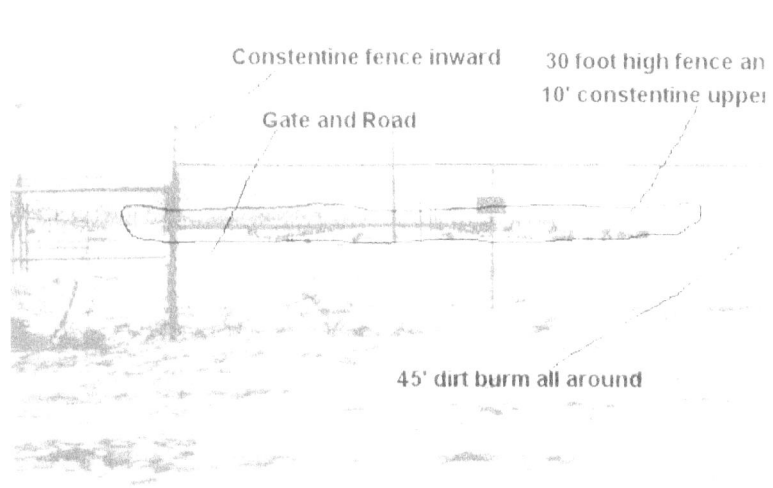

If you are just starting out on your own, it would be good to take some consideration as to picking your place to live. Do you want to live close to where you work or can you handle a commute? Should you live predominantly to the east or west of where you work? Are your professional skills in demand in the country or rural areas or are your skills relegated to the city?

Here are a few of my takes on these questions. If you live close to where you work, chances are good that you will have to live in a more densely populated area which are notoriously areas to be escaped from in the event of an emergency. The more densely populated the area is that you have to traverse, the higher the potential for encounters with predators looking for victims. Avoid people that you don't know.

If you choose to commute, then you are geographically separated from your home and, by logical extension, your family. If you are at work when a situation arises, you will have to slug through the dangers while your family is left without you to help protect them on short notice; also not good.

If you choose to live to the east of where you work, realize that you will not have the sun in your eyes during your morning or evening commute. Live to the west and you'll have the sun glare to deal with twice a day every workday, increasing your chances of getting in a car accident or doing long-term damage to your eyes. It's not really a survival type aspect of choosing where to live, but it is a small consideration.

If your skills are in demand in both rural and urban areas, give some degree of preference to the rural area. Chances are less that you would have to flee a rural area than the pandemonium of a large city riot. You may find home prices are not as high as they are in the city, and you may even be able to get a bit of land in addition to a home. Even one acre can be very productive if properly cultivated. In the event of societal breakdown, it might be a good thing to have the real estate required to feed yourself, not to mention the prospects of having an independent well as your water source. You might even consider accepting a lower salary to take advantage of the benefits a rural home affords.

> *What-2-Do?: Your best way out of a dangerous area is to not be in it in the first place. However, if you find yourself in need to traverse a dangerous or violent area, keep in mind how animals in the wild travel. They observe before they move. They cover short distances and stop to observe again. They repeat this pattern until they get to where they want to go remaining alert to as many dangers and pitfalls as they can possibly detect. We would do well to learn from animals rather than blindly trampling about exposed in open spaces. Study multiple escape routes now and get to know the area.*

• Organization

Organizing is not everyone's strong suit. If it is not yours, find some way to cure it fast. You will need some decent organizational skills if you are to be prepared for the difficult situations that life will invariably throw your way. Managing resources, whether people, time or materials, is a skill that will be of paramount importance in difficult times. One great way to begin developing these skills is to ignore your own perceived weaknesses and throw yourself into the situation with energy and determination.

Ask anyone who completed basic training in our armed services and they will tell you that they found themselves doing things they didn't know they could do, that they were stronger than they thought they were and they dealt with adversity much better than their counterparts in civilian life. Don't think too much. Just act. One of the best axioms I have ever heard came from a Marine friend:

> ***What-2-do***; It is much better to charge ahead with a half-ass plan than to try and write "The Perfect Plan." You'll never have any time to execute it and it'll probably go out the window once the enemy does something you didn't expect. Just have an objective, a somewhat decent plan and the drive to jump into the fray and start working it.

You plan is your strategy. The changes you have to make while implementing your strategy are tactics. Come up with a strategy and make tactical adjustments along the way to accommodate the prior unknowns as they are discovered.

Here is NETT
So where do we start? Well, your neighbors are the ones most likely to be in the same boat as you when the trouble starts, so it would probably be best to start with them. If you are new to your neighborhood, introduce yourself to your neighbors in a friendly atmosphere. Have a cookout, a pool party, whatever. Just start socializing at the most local level. As you build a rapport, start including preparedness into the conversation; introduce them to the underlying principles and the know-how required for self-reliance. You will fairly quickly learn who you can relate with and incorporate into your plans.

Do not go overboard, however. Your enthusiasm for preparedness may be misconstrued as extremism by people ignorant of the concepts of self-reliance, and there are more people that fit this description in the United States than you think. So many have been addicted to entitlements that they have not been taught nor have the impetus to learn how to be 100% self-sufficient. Keep the conversation light and avoid the politically or religiously incendiary language that commonly gets people labeled as nuts.

Once you have a better idea which people are likely to help during tough times, start talking about what; would you all do if "X" were to happen. Come up with the most likely contingencies that could affect your area and start planning for those things mentioned in this chapter, primarily water, food and security.

> *CAUTION: There are people in the United States that have a real and palpable resistance to the common citizen being anything but dependent upon the government, for anything. Many carry microphones and cameras, and they have become so biased in their work that their profession now ranks as low in credibility and respectability as ambulance chasers and the politicians for whom they carry water. Be wary of sweet sounding journalists looking to cover your preparedness efforts. You are not set in a court of law and you have no compunction to treat them as if innocent until proven guilty. Do not let their agendas thwart your efforts and do not grant them the satisfaction. Don't be impolite to them or give them any material that they can selectively edit to make you appear to be some kind of extremist or nut case. That is the kind of thing that could plausibly land you on some domestic terrorist suspect list. You do not want that kind of scrutiny.*

You might have the opportunity to work with a local business. It's not like the economy is currently roaring, but you may find a few business partners willing to support your efforts. They might not offer monetary or material support, but can they spare some storage space in a strategic location? Will they allow you in an emergency to use their parking lot as a staging or distribution area? Granted, you will need to have a large scale operation set up for these ideas to take flight, but you can do it and you can convince others they have it within them to help. You may even approach them from a smaller scale as well, such as allowing you to store a bear trail cache at a business along your route of egress. The worst they can do is say no to you.

> **What-2-Do?:** *You may want to include members of your church, synagogue or mosque. Talk with your religious leaders and see if they want to provide space or services for the neighborhood effort since many people will be showing up on their doorsteps when needs start to exceed supply. Establishing a food pantry can start small and grow over time. You don't need to cross the finish line overnight, but you do need to start somewhere. Asking a congregation to donate a can or two of some basic staples can start the ball rolling.*

The best preventive measure to avoid anarchy following a disaster is for city officials to have planned before a problem happened. Having water, shelter and emergency food available in sufficient quantities is absolutely essential to promote domestic tranquility. This requires heavy planning, and most cities do not want to spend money they do not even have to hire someone to do it. They most certainly would rather gamble with your safety and hope the emergency will not happen. It is up to you to take the initiative to ensure your own wellbeing.

If you must travel, mix with the street people, don't wear fancy or bright color clothes. Don't stand out. Move with the crowd and disappear. Moving at night might be an un-natural time to travel.

In the Next chapter, I will discuss how to get out of the city by planning and using Bear Trails. Bears travel and live in areas where they leave a stash of food. They come back to it when they want their food. This lets them roam about further from their den. This is how I will show you to plan.

Chapter 3

Bear Trails

Planning your escape!

Now here we go into the survival stuff, let's work out your plan to leave the city behind for a Place of refuge.

First, you will need a map of your area, topo (topographic) or use the computer, look at the city where you live. I like going to use Google Earth for this planning step.

Take a good look all around where you live, start looking for a place of refuge about 50 miles out. Now, if the 50-mile area is next to another city or is still populated keep drawing this circle further out until you can find a place that is secluded. If you cannot find such a place you have a big problem in the order of survival. Nowhere to go? If there is a small place somewhere that is rural, you can bet that everybody else will be heading for this place too, by design or accident. Not good! You need to be alone or in a small group for better safety. This is called, escape and evasion techniques. Don't fight! Get out of the city and hide. You can't win a fire fight with our government troops. They have been too well trained in the Iraq war in any kind of city containment.

31

My idea of having lots of guns and ammo to fight whoever is a real good way to die real fast when you leave the city. First, get out of the city during times of anarchy, roving gangs, and whatever comes your way in order to survive. Use the anarchy as a decoy to move out. You will need to be as stealthy as possible, and pray a lot. Avoid all people, normal travel routs, take the impossible routs that no one will take.

Second, now that you have found a place to run to; you will need a plan on how you are going too get there, and how are you going to gather up your family and friends on the way? It would be great if we have advanced warning so that you can just drive there. I don't think that will happen as the highways will become parking lots and military will be all over them. You can be sure it will not come over the local news when it is best to leave.

So we'd better plan on walking out with your pull carts, and backpacks and if we get a chance to drive, great, but don't count on it. Having a CB radio or a walkie-talkie during this time of anarchy can be a great stress relief, use them to coordinate the extractions of family members who need to find you later. They will work if they have batteries. (Be sure to have a solar charger.) They are good for short distances or line of sight waves only. You can get hand held short wave, such as the police have, that will work on a longer distances. The disadvantage of this is everyone will hear you and what you are saying. So, make up code names for people and places etc.

Communications will alleviate a lot of trouble in finding people and developing a plan as the emergency develops. Don't spare any expense in this area. Most importantly, being able to talk to loved ones during any crisis will help calm everyone down. You must be able to talk to the kids if they are in school, and to mom at home or work and to dad. Everyone should have the family plan deeply rooted in their brain as to where each family member will assemble first. It may take a few days to get where you are going this is not a problem if you have prepared your bear trails.

The first assembly area should contain backpacks for everyone and prepare you for the first night or two. You will then pick up other needed supplies along the way. Each car should have an emergency backpack for walking to the ground zero meeting place as your car will be useless on the freeway parking lots or streets; change of clothes, shoes, equipment and water. Wherever you are, if you are prepared others around you will need your help too and may follow you out, so plan for them. Practice this plan of yours a few times, makes sure it works.

Leaving your places of work using roads that are jammed with cars heading out can slow or stop any progress of assembling. Plan alternate routes, and if you have to walk, how long will it take you, you don't want people to leave you behind, unless necessary and meet up at another assemble area further out. That's why it is so important to have a radio to communicate and make alternate plans if you have to on the spot.

What about your kids in school? Maybe one is in one area school and another is across town in another school? This is your biggest nightmare, extraction plan with the kids. The only way out of this problem is to talk with school principal/or school board to allow kids to get out of school during these emergencies. Get rid of the "Lock down" rule. It is going to be frightening for any kid during this time without communication from parents. Figure out a way to communicate with them. Be sure they will follow your plan to get out of school.

Due to the recent shootings in the schools, this lock down and prison camp idea has real force now. The only way out of this problem, in my mind, is to teach the kids at home or tell them during a real lock down it is ok to break a window and run like HELL.

The schools have orders to "lock down" the school and police will be posted at the front door, if the police are available. Hopefully, the police will be so busy doing something else that the schools will not have police protection and the busses will not be used either due to traffic problems or confusion. Confusion on their part is your best weapon to escape.

No one, I mean NO ONE is allowed in or out during "Lock-Down." The children will need to be freed in some manner. If not, they will go to an undisclosed "*place of safety*" and maybe then, you can pick them up if you know where this place of safety is located. Maybe it will be a camp of some sort that you must submit yourself to their control and be relocated to wherever the government says. It is up to you and friends as to how you and other parents handle this problem.

Here in Utah is one of our "places of safety", it is a concentration camp, located west of Utah Lake. Anyone can drive by it. There are many places in every town that can be used as well, old warehouses etc. Hopefully, by this time you are all together and ready to make the trip out of town. You will need to prepare this trip in advance of actually using it. Practice! Practice! Practice! Drill! and then drill again.

After you have located a way out of town you may want to become a Johnny Apple Seed type. planting herbs and other berries etc. Map out the route you plan to walk then take an eye to eye look at it. If it still seems good, let's go to work. You will need to plant or seed along this trail with all kinds of berries, herbs (garlic), potatoes/onions and anything else you think might grow there along the way, anything that can grow naturally. Find out where the water is. Plan to filter or purify the water if you think you need to.

Take a look at the high ground for observation, protecting you or that may detect you, by others. This is called escape. If you need to hide, you know where to go. Stock pile equipment, plan to build a small shelter (rope and plastic/tarps) to keep you from the weather and in case of nuclear fall-out. Be sure to have on hand Iodide pills for this. Remember food must be stored underground if possible that is completely hidden from view, or it will be discovered by others.

This is how to do it with P.V.C. Pipe. Now you are ready to develop your "trail." Here is what you will need to get. P.V.C. Pipe; Use 4" to 6" pipe, about two feet long, glue one cap on one end of a two-foot section. Now, you're ready to stuff your stuff.

We want to store food, equipment, tools, guns/ammo (for hunting wild game) and water into the tube and then screw the top cap on. Spray paint the top cap or write with a black marker what is in the tube, For example, use blue for water, green for food, red for guns, brown for equipment and tools, etc, you get the idea. Make sure the family understands what the colors mean. Don't forget the chest freezer, barrels dug in ground idea too, as this might help to store bigger stuff, like sleeping bags, tents. It's a lot of work with only a shovel or a post-hole digger, but it is worth the effort if you need it.

For the food items if they are not freeze dried you must take out the O^2 in each tube. Let's say we have a granola blend or trail mix we want to store. Pour the entire food blend into a paper sack. Crumple up a newspaper and place it at the bottom of the tube. Then you add a small piece of dry ice, about the size of a corn kernel, drop it onto the newspaper. Hold the tube open end up and let the dry ice push the Oxygen out. Crumple up a newspaper and shove it down on top of the dry ice. Wait a few seconds and then loosely stuff your paper sacks of food into the tube and let the dry ice push all the Oxygen out of the sacks and tube. Oxygen is what causes food to go bad. This procedure will take some time. When enough time has passed, light a match and hold it over the top of the tube, when the match goes out (because no Oxygen) we are ready to place the screw top cap on. Don't close it all the way, let the dry ice push the remaining Oxygen out first or it could expand and break the tube. When you think the dry ice is gone, then tighten the cap and place a little PVC glue around its edge. You must be able to open this food source someday so don't get carried away with the glue.

Drive out along your trail and use a post-hole digger/shovel to dig a hole to hide and plant these storage tubes (vertical or horizontal) where you think you will need them. Take the family with you so they can get an idea as to where they are too. You need to plan how far you think you can walk before you will need this storage food and water, which will depend on who is coming with you and ages and special needs of those. Water and food are first to dig and maybe protection equipment stuff. Then a sleeping bag or wool blanket, survival blanket, cords and plastic/tarp to use for shelter. If you have a river to cross or other obstacle you will need tools and nails and ropes to cross it, plant them near the river and use them to make what you need to cross and then replant them when you are done on the other side. Who knows, you may want to return and need to cross. Figure out what you will need and where you will need it, and plant it there.

How do you find it again? By leaving yourselves clues. The Indians would dig and leave stuff and then write the clue on a rock or tree to find it again. You need to design your own unique clues. Here's how:

Write on the rock or a tree how to find your stuff and what's planted, use codes or symbols so others won't know what is there.

For example.
Stand in front of the starting mark, go 92 degrees for 15. Now, how to figure what that says. If you don't confuse someone else who might be reading this, they could steal your whole supply. We need to confuse them, you know that for every marking of degrees you add or subtract 10 degrees, and for 15 it could mean feet, yards or paces only you know. If someone else reads your code and starts to dig they will be way off the mark.

What if someone is following you? They appear, just as you are digging up your stuff. Always plant a dummy stash or an additional food supply near this one. You give them your stuff and cry about it and when they are gone, dig up another stash. You're alive and you win.

I've gone back into my stashes in Montana after five years and the trail mix was still good. The gold coins were still good too. You might consider stashing trade goods too, like little bottles of Whisky, cigarettes, candy, and coffee etc. These trade items work well for just about anything you may need to trade for.

Chapter 4 is going to explain how to protect your water either in the outback or in the city. Water is going to be a major concern for either place.

Chapter 4

Protecting Your Water Supply

This will be one of the major problems you will face, either in the back woods or in the City; you must have clean drinkable water.

The Department of Homeland Security, your state government and your city or town managers are not prepared in any credible extent to protect our most vulnerable and highest priority resource; our water supply. The people we elect to lead do not think it is a judicious use of public funds to protect water supplies from any kind of terrorist attack, industrial catastrophe or even from an electrical grid failure. Folks, this is not good.

Wherever you live, you must have water to drink. Just a few days without it and you will die. It is that simple. A terrorist could use any of a number of biological agents to contaminate a stream which drains into a lake or any one of our city's reservoirs. Even farmers who have a collection pond to water stock or crops could be contaminated as well.

Our water supply is our most vulnerable resource to protect against a terrorist attack. It is our largest and softest target. Drinking water is gathered from streams and rivers which are openly drained into lakes and reservoirs. For the most part, our waterways are unprotected. You can fly over them, boat on them, swim in them and when no one is looking, dump your trash in them. Contaminate a stream as it goes on to flow into the lakes and contaminate them as well. A coordinated attack on several water systems is a nightmare terrorism scenario.

If we lose our water supply, it triggers a cascading failure in which we lose everything including our economic base. Millions of people will perish in just a few days unless we find some way to bring in industrial amounts of water. The only organization able to come even close to fulfilling this effort is the Armed Services and you can be sure that rations will be in place. If the shortages are severe enough, you can expect rioting and its' ultimate counterpart; Martial law. These are very real possibilities.

Two things will exacerbate the situation; high population density and high temperature climates. If you live in a heavily populated area, such as Los Angeles, New York City, San Francisco, Chicago or Houston, the sheer number of people needing potable water will overwhelm any logistical chain we could hope to establish. Hot climate areas, such as Las Vegas, Phoenix, Miami, Orlando, Dallas and New Orleans will require more water per capita.

Desalinization plants could produce industrial amounts of fresh water, but they are not prevalent in the United States at the time of writing. Desalinization plants could serve as a great hedge against contaminated water supplies since it relies on the bay, gulf or ocean waters to provide process input, and the bigger the body of water, the harder it is to contaminate. It is more expensive than wells, rivers and reservoirs for everyday fresh water requirements, but it is feasible.

Those that do exist must clear social and political hurdles to get online. For instance, environmentalists effectively stalled work on the desalinization plant on the east side of Tampa Bay due to objections arising from increased salinity levels at the plant's discharge points. That is what is supposed to happen! These objections would have been more appropriately raised before the plant was built, but hey—it wasn't the environmentalist's money, so why would they care?

The problems were overcome and the desalinization plant now produces 25 million gallons of fresh water per day; a full 10% of the region's needs. Imagine if all seaboard cities had such a drought proof and reproducible fresh water production capability! It is great to have, but what if you are not on a municipal water system?

You need to think bigger and longer when it comes to your personal water requirements. The 72-hour figure will not be sufficient for the needs of self-sufficiency. You are going to need a way to find, collect or produce enough water to supplement (or better, replenish) your stored water.

Ignoring this problem can make you "go away." Start small and work your way up in terms of storage capacity. Start purchasing your soft drinks in 2-liter bottles. When emptied, wash them out, fill them and store them in your attic or crawlspace. Each one will give you a day's worth of this needed resource with zero additional up-front costs.

You can ramp up your storage capacity with a ten dollar, six gallon plastic water can (BPA free, of course!) available at your local Walmart or via their website. Each one of these will give you at least a week's worth of water.

If you are after the Grand Behemoth of water storage, you can purchase water cistern tanks well into the thousand gallon range. Keeping that much water fresh for long term storage will present some new problems, but they are not insurmountable, even on modest budgets.

Unless the people do something now to protect themselves, the devastation and death will be unspeakable. Sure, you can just ignore this problem and hope it does not happen, much like the mayor. That is one way to deal with problems, ignore them, or say, the cost is too much.

Here is my personal plan for water survival. <u>Do something!!</u>

Home survival; you will need to purchase a 1,000 gallon tank or larger, one inch plastic pipe and fittings. Place the tank under one corner of the house and use the rain gutter to collect water and fill the tank. The tank water can be used for toilets, watering the lawns or gardens, but when you need to drink it, it will be there.

My home in the mountains, not much to look at but it is paid for and functional. This, in and of itself, is a great water supply for those city dwellers who are low on water. If you have to use it to drink, be sure you have a good filter on the pipe and you may want to boil it too. While the tank is sitting there full of water, pour in a cup of Clorox or use a pool pill to keep it smelling and looking good.

Water, you must have water. If you do not have access to a well, drill one. Pool the church members' money, friends, business whatever. Drill a Well and use solar to pump it. This could save hundreds of lives during any kind of an emergency. If you can get the city manager to wake up, demand that they drill a well at every school in the area. Build a small building around the well, and place solar panels for the pumping. Also store pipeline and when you're ready you can construct the pipe from a storage tank to a larger line of at least 50 facets on the pipe. People can come and get water. This will prevent riots, anarchy and death.

Homeland Security gives out a lot of money to cities for planning for an emergency. The problem is that the police purchase snow mobiles, scuba equipment, boats, four wheelers, etc. etc. as they did in Salt Lake City. None of these items will provide any help during a real emergency. They are nothing less than Police Toys, they got for free. The police and city managers need real planning, and they have not taken the time to do it. Maybe purchase equipment, like a well drilling rig or use it to pay someone to drill a few wells around town for an emergency use. City officials and police are so far out of the thinking of an emergency it's scary. They think short term, overnight type of events. They need to think Anarchy for at least one or two weeks and longer if you can. No water, No electricity, and what problems this would have on their city, and they haven't done it. Then you will have a city program that will save lives. Anything less is short sided planning and will not help anyone, vote them out and get someone in who will plan.

This basic idea can be planned for churches, or large factory buildings. It can also be a requirement for all new large building permits. The only way to have good clean water is to place a well in the ground. There are only so many permits in an area for a well. Pass some kind of proposal that will give permission to drill, if it is only used for emergency, not to be taxed. Maybe you can use a tax deduction for corporations to use this plan for the people in the area.

If there are enough wells in all the schools, it will decrease, if not stop, the anarchy of people who will kill to get a drink of water. We have read the newspapers about this actually happening. Schools could have solar-power for electricity, and communications as well as food storage to prevent anarchy. If you can't prevent it, then you must prepare yourself to live in it . . .

How do you get water out of a well when you don't have electricity? If you have a well then you must purchase a solar system to get the water into your home. The next idea is to improvise a well-bucket of my design.

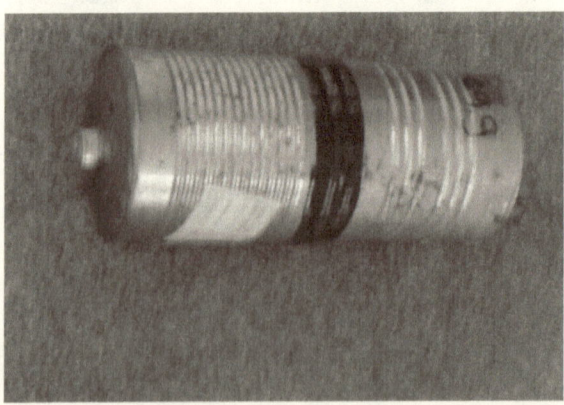

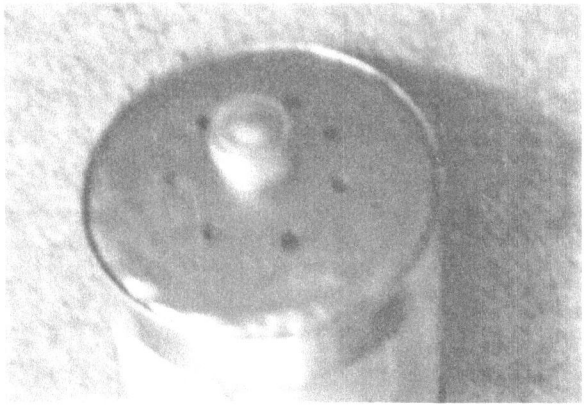

Start out with two coffee cans if you have a large well or smaller cans for smaller well diameter. Take one can and punch 6 holes in the bottom and one in the middle. Use a two inch bolt, to hold down two rubber bladders inside the can, when the bucket is lowered into the well and hits the water the holes and the bladder will allow the water to rise up into the bucket and when you lift the bucket the weight of the water will close the bladder over the holes and hold water.

On the center bolt be sure to add a lot of washers for weight which will help pull the bucket down into the water.

If you have 55 gal drums of water stored, it is very labor intensive to keep that water healthy. You need to chlorinate it regularly or change the water every few months.

I hope this helps you to plan on what will work for you to have plenty of water. The next Chapter 5 is about how much worth is a 72 hr. survival kit. I don't think much of it as in most cases an emergency will be a lot Longer. Plan for at least two weeks, Minimum.

Chapter 5

72 hour Survival Kits

This is a false security blanket, it is too little and you need some
additional planning that will take you at least 2 weeks.
The economy is crashing and when it's gone,
It will last longer than 72 hours.
The best survival kit will be your training and planning.

I have watched the purchasing of 72 hour kits for the last 15 years
or so, and now it has been proposed by Homeland Security as well.
What makes anyone believe that an emergency will only last for 72
hours? If all we need is 72 hours, heck, we have that much stuff in
the house already.

Seems that it is just a sales gimmick so, I ask you, why have one?
It is a waste of your money. But if you want one at least follow my
recommendation and purchase what you need, not what the boy
scouts say you need.

The problem I see with this little or nothing kit is that it gives you the
idea that you are prepared for something, when in fact you are not
prepared for anything. It is in fact a false security blanket because

relying on it just might kill you. Now, If you put it in your car for a short time emergency, that might work well.

One of the main problems with these kits is that they are prepared by boy scouts or someone like that, or anyone trying to make a buck. They have *not* been prepared by anyone who actually understands what your individual needs might be for emergencies.

You are the expert here, you know what you need. Get a back pack and do it yourself and save a lot of money. But when you get right down to an emergency kit, that kit is your mind. Your training is the only item that you can take with you no matter where you are. The better trained you are the better your chances for survival. Think about it, why does the military train for every situation that they may face? To survive any emergency is determined by your own knowledge for a good outcome. A 72 hour kit is nice for a few hours or in your car.

Let's, go over a few things to help you design your survival for home and in your car. I have given you some points in the previous chapters. Now I get specific in preparing for home emergency problems.

First, look at what you/family might be facing. Let us plan for the worst and if the disaster is less than that, great! We will have more than enough to survive. Figure on this: No electricity, no phones, no water, no police or firefighters, no transportation. Everything has stopped. You must depend on yourself and each family member must do the same. This requires a plan, so that each person even if they are alone and separated, will know what the others are doing in this emergency. That is, following the plan. Most important . . . following the plan!

So, what is the plan? Take each person in the family and determine where they are during the day. How far are they from home? Is it possible for each member to get home or do we need to find a common meeting place and then move out from there? Are there any special problems to overcome in traveling home or in meeting somewhere? Are there any special medical problems that need to be addressed? If the kids are in school, you may have a real bad problem in that the schools are commanded to lock down. Thus, you will not be able to get the kids from school. They are forced to get on the bus and go to a place of safety that no one knows the location. How do you find them again? I don't know. Maybe, you can get with the school board and make other rules. Maybe the police will be so busy that they will not be able to enforce this rule on parents at the school. Somehow you have to get the kids or teach them to do whatever they need to do to get out and run.

Once you have written down exactly what you need to do, practice it. Drive it so each person can see where the other family members will be and what they will face. Write down what you might need in the way of food, water, clothes, protection, and equipment. For example; ropes, binoculars, walkie-talkies, maybe a rubber raft to get across a river. Each of you will have completely different needs to survive so you can meet up later.

Now you have an idea as to what you may face, how far you will have to travel and how long it will take you to meet up with family. The next step is to prepare your backpack kit and be sure each person has it handy. Plan what you will need at home or at the meeting area, so you can have things stored there, too. If you have to leave the area, make a plan for that.

Security is a big part of the plan. Don't plan on fighting your way out. That is a no win situation. Escape and evasion is the only way to survive. Traveling in a male dominated group might give you some protection. People will kill you if they think you have food and water that they need. Desperation turns good people into crazy people very quickly. It is going to be dangerous. If you move out during the time of most confusion, it might give you a head start. This takes organization and planning on your part. There will not be any law and order except individual morale and the longer it goes on the worse it might get.

Make sure you have some kind of radio contact with each other. The events are stressful enough without compounding the stress with questions about where your wife is or your kids. Be able to talk to them.

Make a plan and don't rely on just a 72 hour kit to save the day. It is too little too late. A 72 hour kit will not last you long enough you will need more food storage than that. If you plan on spending a few extra dollars every month it will all come together. Eating freeze dried commercial survival food just does not taste good. Better to have food children will eat. Add survival food to a stressful situation just adds more stress on your kids and overloads their mental terror.

Chapter 6

Food Storage

Should be called, Stocking Your Pantry
Or Self-sufficiency

Your food storage is based on what you eat, what you have in the cupboards. We think of food storage as a survival food that we store and will not eat during an emergency, emergency FOOD is a four letter word. When I mention food storage people go into shock and a dumb look comes over their face. If we really wanted to have food storage we would be self-sufficient by growing and raising everything we eat . . . But if you like to have a garden then grow what the Indian's called the 3 sisters: Dent Corn, Beans, and Squash.

Stop thinking survival food as storage, think of it as just filling up your pantry with what your family usually eats every month. Don't by one item, buy the whole case it is that simple. When you go to the store for a bottle of ketchup, get a case of it. Don't purchase single items, purchase a case and then build on the case lot stuff and it is cheaper in the long run to buy in bulk. Get 25 or 50, 6-gal buckets and store 5 buckets of pancake mix and a few cases of 1-gal syrup bottles. Purchase what you like to eat, that's the key in a bad situation.

One of the best survival foods, well balanced in fiber, proteins and carb's is nothing else than a wheat bread, peanut butter and jam sandwich.

If you can find some of your favorite food products in freeze dried, great store them for an emergency. Don't forget to buy survival seeds. This will prevent you from making the mistakes like your neighbors who are trying to purchase freeze dried food storage package deals and when the time comes, will starve to death as they will not eat it or there is no water to re-hydrate it or a way to cook it.

A few problems with food storage programs is you don't have the variety of food that you are used to eating. Anyone who has raised kids knows that they will eat what they know, change that diet and you will have a riot on your hands. Also with kids in this very stressful situation, changing their food habits just ads to the stress. Make sure you have a lot of happy foods to feed them, Birthday cakes, sweets, coco, and the like. What do we do when we get stressed? Go out to dinner. Look for happy foods.

Children might do well in staying busy like planting the Garden as these three did.

In an emergency, stress is a major factor of life, don't compound it with a new diet of rice cakes or foods that you don't like and will not eat. If you have a lot of wheat and all of a sudden begin to eat it, you might just kill yourself with clogged drain pipes. You need food that you like and are used to eating and a good variety of it to stay healthy both mentally and physically.

Once your food pantry is full, begin to enlarge it with freeze dried and bulk items like beans, rice and wheat. Use your canning jars to store meats and greens from your greenhouse. And don't forget a case or two of vitamins, medical supplies, cough drops, ear drops, eye drops, etc. One way to make sure you have them is purchase a bottle for home use and a case for the pantry.

We have talked about this before and that is your *psychological happy meals.* If you purchase something for home get a case for the pantry that makes the family feel good. This way you get the right foods that you like for those moments of deep stress. For example; cakes, frosting, goodies, all kinds of candies and popcorn. It will really help when you are depressed or a birthday comes up, you will have a cake ready to go. Even if you are camping outside your home, you must have some happy meals. Believe me when I say this, I was on C-rations and meal time was depressing to say the least, and they didn't taste good either. The psychological health of the family is very, important, have music, games etc. Keep your humor going strong. If you are with a group, do this in the group with dances and that . . . BE HAPPY.

If you use plastic 6-gal buckets, don't store the food directly into the bucket, purchase food grade plastic containers, NOT garbage sacks. Why not use Garbage sacks? They are not made with the idea of food being placed in them, they are not sterile and the bag itself is made with chemicals that will decay or leach into the food. Store your food items in a cool, dry place. A special room in the basement or dig a root cellar is best. Store your veggies from the greenhouse that I know you have built for this purpose.

In the root cellar you need to have an old chest freezer dug into the ground to keep other foods really cool and fresh.

Pemmican,

The all-purpose wilderness food! All meat must be completely dried, stiff, hard and dry. This may take a few days or a week or so in the sun and have a lot of Morton's Meat salt cure. Dry your meat in the sun and then pound it into dust. Use a hammer or whatever you have, make a powder of the meat. The amount of meat you now have is very small from what you started with, it reduces way down. Thus, 5 or 6 pounds of good roast will reduce down to about one pound.

Mix 1 lb of fat, I like to use lard, to 1 lb of meat, mix it well and let it cool into strips of meat, which is called Pemmican. If you want to spice it up some here are a few hints, dry and crush some wild berries, raisins, oatmeal, pine nuts or peanuts etc. into the mixture. Me. I like to add a little smoke flavor and some Mexican hot sauce, it is up to you. I like this much better than jerky or smoking some meat.

Your food storage plan should be what you can make, dry or smoke as food storage.

Purchase equipment so that you can process food like this for years . . . It just might be a very long time before the lights get turned on.

Raw, cut onions will absorb all kinds of toxins and bacteria so leave one out on a plate in your storage area, changing it frequently. Never eat an onion that has been cut and sitting in the fridge or on the counter, it has absorbed all the impurities in the air. It will become poisonous even in a zip lock bag. Never eat onions from anywhere where they have been sitting out, like a hot dog bar. *Left over onions are* poisonous.

If our government wants to take control of us, if they take all the food, we will come running like dogs to the bowl and we will do anything they want for food. Watch FEMA take our guns and food we will be helpless. Government will have to take the mark of the beast to survive.

So, now, Chapter 7, you have your food storage now let discuss Emergency water and your pantry planning.

Chapter 7

Emergency Water and Home Pantry Planning

Water will become the most important item to store or collect for any emergency. You must store enough for your family and the neighbors who failed to plan. The worst thing you can do is waste good drinking water. Don't waste water; it is for drinking and drinking only.

Anarchy, civil disturbances and even murder will occur by people who can't get water or food for themselves and their children. Your best friends will turn on you for water and food as has been shown in a recent calamity where a man shot and killed his sister for a bag of ice. If you have it you must share it with others, or risk being killed for it. Homeland security has given millions of dollars to states, police and fire departments to help them purchase emergency preparedness items, they have used this money for toys; four-wheeler, snow mobiles, scuba equipment.

Nothing that could really help in an emergency with 1000's of people in need.

The best way to store water is with a separate water tank in the back yard, under your rain gutter. Next, I believe that everyone should have a greenhouse in the back yard and keep it in use year round. It will more than pay for itself with real food. A large, well ventilated food storage room in the home is a must. Set aside one room in the home for your pantry. I like calling it a pantry, because this is food you eat every day. Storage is freeze dried stuff that is for a longer period of time and yes, you should have this type of food too. It is easier to stock a pantry than a food storage plan.

This plan works on the bases that when you need a can of this or that, you will purchase a case of it. Keep in your pantry at least 2 cases of the things you like to eat. This is a great idea to remember. You will have all that you like to eat, instead of stuff you hate and will not eat.

The psychological reason for this is simple. You and the family are under a lot of stress right now. Food is a stress reducer, it relaxes children and adults, it makes a lot of problems seem less if you can eat foods that your family uses. Your favorite meal or whatever, for me it is in the morning having a cup of coffee or hot chocolate. Have a large supply of goodies to help the kids think that this is not so bad. A psychological drain is to sit in the dark, so have some kind of lighting in your home. This is wonderful to lower stress, but if you are concerned with gangs, cover the windows.

Having solar power to plug into for a nightly movie is a really great way to help the psychological and emotional stress of the emergency. We think of the body of food, shelter and water, but the emotional stress of an emergency can kill you too.

Once you have a large pantry of food, then start building the long term food items and don't forget to supply your home with planting seeds. Planting seeds for sprouting or for growing food later on, if the emergency has destroyed our fragile economy, would be a life saver too. I have canned survival garden seeds; go to my web site for ordering.

Don't think for one moment that a 72 hour kit is all you need. Don't for one moment place your confidence in just having a 72 hour kit. This lazy idea may just kill you and your loved ones. You need a lot more than just 72 hours; you need to think long term. Everyone can survive for 72 hours with what they have in the home.

Think of all that you will need for two weeks or two years without electricity, water gas and heating. If you live where you have cold winters be sure and have a wood heating device installed in the home. You will need this for warmth and cooking your food. Most of what you need is a no brainer, you will know what you need if you sit down and think about it.

You will not be able to drive anywhere, no phones will work. The home refrigerator will not work, the toilet will not work, no water for two weeks. Plan for this and you just might make it. The next step is to plan for an escape from any kind of anarchy, sickness and filth living in town. The first year will be the hardest after that it's fun, right?

Homeland Security has told us to plan on getting out of the cities because we need too and if the Army tells us to leave because of a gas line leak, toxins, and danger of an explosion or whatever you will have to go. You will have your choice of going with them or if you are prepared, to go somewhere on your own. You must realize that the city is the worst place to be to survive an emergency, once you believe this the better your planning will be.

If you are on a budget, store bread making, peanut butter and jam; next rolled oats and honey for food.

Sleeping Bags and 10 extra
Metal Match
Wood to burn
Mullein charcole
Outdoor cooking pans
Shower bag
Cleaning soaps
Candles,/flash lights/solar
Solar Radio
FM Walkie-talkies
Tents/ tarps
Ropes
Fishing Stuff
Boots for all/winter and summer
Warm Clothes/ socks
Buckets
Water Purification
Canteens
Solar Flash Lights
Steel Wool, 4-00
55gal drum for sanitation
Surgical tubing
Make a well bucket

List of Food Storage	۵۵۵	NOTES

If you are on a budget, store bread making, peanut butter and jam; next rolled oats and honey.

All kinds of canned meats/fish
Freeze dried meats
Hunting supplies for meat.
Supplies for, smoking,
Beans, all kinds and barely
Canned and freeze dried Vegetable for soups etc.
Garden Seeds and equipment
Soup base broths
Wheat,
The 3 sisters, corn, squash and beans.
Happy meals and lots of them
Hot & cold drinks
Juice drinks
Hard candy
Medical supplies
Speacial Equipment/tools
Garden tools
Tarps/rope
Duck tape
Toilet tissue
Diapers
Wet Wipes
Binoculars
Games
Refereance Books, how to
Knives, for Trade item
Cigeretts for trade
Small whiskey etc. for trade.

One last point, some people want to use 5-gal plastic buckets for storage, I like the idea but you should understand that placing raw food in a plastic trash can is not the thing to do. Trash—can plastic is the wrong plastic to use as it is toxic material and designed to disintegrate in the landfill. Use food grade container plastic, zip-lock or commercial and a dry packet with it.

Think about taking your family out camping for a two week period and what you will need and take a few things you just want to relieve stress.

Most of these supplies are listed and explained why you need them and how to use them.

Chapter 8

Emergency Planning

What Might Happen? This is the big question isn't it?
And the next is, will it happen to me? The answer is, YES!

If we only knew what might happen to us in the future we would know how to prepare our emergency plan, wouldn't we? We don't know, but be sure something will happen, so we are at a point of *our best guess*. Will it be nuclear, will it be a terrorist attack, and will it be a natural disaster, or biological or just some air borne sickness, like the bird flu. Whatever it is, it will bring on Anarchy to your streets, the bigger the city the bigger the problem. Earthquakes—This could affect millions of people in a far reaching way. It could affect our electricity grid and close it down over the entire state and others. It could disrupt the transportation of all our food goods. No water, no electricity, no law and order and you have anarchy.

Biological Attack—This could spread panic and deaths over a large part of any city as well, and without damaging any of our physical structures. Our industry is a big price for anyone if they can take it without damaging it. It would also create a mental break down that would be worse than the attack itself.

Dirty Bomb-(EMP, Electrical Magnetic Pulse) This could cause a large damaged area and possible radiation sickness death rate, much like a Biological Attack. An EMP could take out the entire Pacific Fleet. This would not be good. After such an attack, whoever is behind it would be sending their Army in next.

Solar Flares—According to a recent study published by Space Weather; The International Journal of Research and Applications, we have a 12% (I think it is much higher from other sources) chance of getting hit with a solar storm so powerful that it could take down the national power grid and yield catastrophic consequences for the *general* population. Just take a look at the flares on Feb. 9th of 2012. Scientist of the Sun says it is going to be a big year. The Sun is about to flip poles as of writing this.

Without going into a large scale section on what could happen to us, let's look at these four areas for now. Any one of them will create Anarchy in your city. Until food and water, and medical help arrive, it will be a complete breakdown of civil authority.

In all five areas of emergency we have one conclusion that comes to my mind and that Is; *anarchy* . . . . Leave the area, leave the infected area. If you look at each problem and how to avoid the problem, it seems that the only way out is to leave to a place of safety.

If this is the case, why would we want to spend thousands of dollars on storage foods that we will leave behind at our home, we can't carry it on our backs to get it out. It must be deposited in a rural area for pick—up later. Hopefully, at a friend's house that lives way out of the area, or pay for a storage unit. These are not great ideas, but there is nothing else you can do.

That being the case, we must plan on an escape route out of the city in order to survive the emergency. We can plan for the trip and also plan what we need to store or have on supply. Now we can use our money in a more proficient manner and purchase equipment rather than tons of wheat for example or other items that will be left behind. What would happen if LA or a major city was destroyed? Maybe an outbreak of some sickness that will cause economic destruction all across this nation. The question is, to what point? It is possible that this could create an emergency that would be catastrophic; no food, no water, no gasoline, no electricity, bank closures, and then anarchy, lawlessness in the streets. Let me say this again, you will have to leave your home to survive. This will give you the highest chance of safety.

If we plan on leaving and we don't have too, GREAT! But if we need to leave and we have placed all our eggs in one basket, our families might be gravely affected by our mistake in judgment. I guess it is up to you. You and you alone will have to live with yourself and heaven help you if you convinced others not to leave and they suffered because of your short mindedness.

The next part should help you plan to leave and let's hope we don't have to.

Family Planner	ΩΩ	Notes
From Dad's work, how many miles?		
How many minutes to drive home?		
How many minutes to walk home?		
From Mom's work, how many miles?		
How many minutes to drive home?		
How many minutes to walk home?		
How else is working from home, same question.		
Kids, in school.		
How many miles to home?		
How long to walk home?		
Do they know the way home?		
Where are parents to meet up with older kids.		
Principals name and phone number.		
Police Chiefs, name and phone number.		
Nett, team name and phone to get the kids.		
Place for children to meet and then walk home?		
Place for children to meet, parents?		
How to talk to each other when phone is not.?		
Walkie-talkie, hidden location (Not in school Locker)		
Dad have change of clothes and back-pack?		
Mom have change of clothes and back-pack?		
School children prepared?		
Food & Water preparation, for each.		
Any Medical?		
First place of safety.		
Second place of safety.		
Planning for children while waiting for parents.		
Special instructions.		
Practice your planning.		

Each car must have a back pack with the driver: shoes, pants, cold weather gear, energy food, binoculars, gun, tarp, rope, FM radio communications, signal mirror, fire starter, map, and specialty needs, medical.

Everyone must have a plan for walking home designed and practiced. A plan to follow that everyone else will know about and know where you will be at any given moment of your travel. A plan should include how to avoid trouble on the way and stay out of sight from trouble around each corner. If you have children in school, this will be your biggest heartache problem. Getting the children out of school and into a safe house, while you are at work will be a big relief. This is one reason why a *Neighborhood Emergency Team* is so important. The only way to do this is to have a neighbor pick them up and care for them until you arrive. The school must be given a signed paper from you, to be on file authorizing them to turn over your child to your neighbor in case of an emergency; this probably will not work with any school. If the school goes into a lock down, no one may be allowed to get their kids. If that happens you and I are in deep trouble. The school is programmed to pick up kids at the school, load them on the bus and drive somewhere to what they consider is a safe spot.

We as parents will not know where that is. Now what do you do . . . . I don't know what to tell you. Change the way the school handles this problem by getting your school board to change the rules, would be my choice, if they don't, those who have realized what is going on may have a plan to shoot the tires off the busses, so they can't transport. Maybe, an all-out assault on the school, by a few fathers to get their kids out. I can't tell you what to do here. You have to get the kids. That is all there is too it. Your children need to be prepared by you, to know what to do and where to find you later if they break out of the school on their own.

Special instruction for kids in school on what to do; what they should plan for or know.

Who calls the school? _____

Who picks them up? _____

Go to a safe house? _____

Where? _____

Phone: _____

Use the rest of the page for any more instructions or planning for your family. To help prevent this type of problem you should get a

Neighborhood Emergency Team started in your area or city. This is a good idea, but it is hard to do because of everyone's attitudes getting in the way of progress. Individuals can volunteer for doing a project and then share with the group. Churches seem to do the best if the minister is in full charge of the operation. It might be that you will depend on one or two families and the rest will have to do their own planning.

Chapter 9

Wilderness Food Planning

Now that we are out in the bush,
how do we plan for our food and water?

This may sound kind of simple, but our greatest learning curve was how to keep foods from spoiling during the summer months and how to use the commercial storage foods stuff we had. There were two major problems in commercial dried foods.

I spent hundreds of dollars on a lot of useless survival foods that no one, not even me, would eat. First, the problem with them is you can't transport them if you are *walking* out of harm's way. Second, if you don't have a large water source, can't re-hydrate them they are useless. These are some real drawbacks to commercial food storage plans. They make you feel good at the time, but when it's time to use it you find out too late that they have some real drawbacks and then it's too late to fix it.

The solution, I arrived at is to live off the land as much as you can. Live like our pioneer grandparents did. They grew beans, corn and squash as well as many other staples, and tended animals. We can carry a lot of seeds to sprout and later grow. Eat soups with beans, rice and whatever you can find for meat. The pioneers and Indians ate a lot of rabbits in stews. I have to laugh when I see these mighty hunters go out carrying the whole city with them in their fifth wheel trailers. Think simple, eat simple and enjoy the trip. When you don't have an electric refrigerator, what do you do to keep your frozen food from spoiling?

It takes some planning before that happens. You will need a few potato sacks, wire bug screen and a large pan (like a large open oil pan). If you have an old cupboard somewhere that is about it. One way to get ready for eating and buying food storage is; start changing your diet somewhat now and what you purchase has to be preserved in such a way you don't need a refrigerator.

Your monthly eating menu should be a part of your long term food storage plan. By changing your daily eating habits to your long term plan, you will begin to purchase foods that will last longer. This is a better idea than a 72 hour kit, believe me.

Not having electricity to run everything in your life is difficult especially when you have grown up with it and then not to have it. This can be a bigger mental problem than it really is. Wow, everything depends on electricity, how in the world did civilization do it before our time?

If you can't preserve it, then you have to pick it when you want it. We found that it is easier to grow it from a greenhouse than it was to purchase it in cans etc. We learned that some things do NOT need refrigeration, just keep them cool. A chest freezer, old refrigerator, dug into the ground can work well in summer and is great in the winter to store food in. It is not a freezer unless you live at the North Pole, however refrigerators are a great way to stash equipment or food that you may walk to when getting out of the cities also.

If you have a stream available you can store food in the water under a shade tree. Place the foodstuff in a potato sack so that the food will not leak into the water and use a net to hold it all. Then tie the net to a rope and the other end to a tree. Drop the net in deep water, a few rocks will hold it down for complete emersion.

Our Refrigerator idea; build a box without walls, have a few shelves in it and place a bucket of water on top with a rag hanging over the four edges. The box is wrapped in a potato sack. The water will be sucked out of the bucket onto the potato sack, as it drips down it cools. The wind comes up and blows through the potato sack and you have an evaporator refrigerator. I used this in Arizona and it worked really well on hot days.

This is an old cupboard that I took the back off and replaced it with a burlap potato sack and I have a large baking pan on top with the burlap inside the pan and hanging down the outside. Fill the pan with water and it will soak down the burlap outside. The wind blows through the burlap and cools the items very well in summer. It works !!! We have kept meat and milk for weeks this way. It really works great.

You may have access to a back-hoe and dig a nice root cellar/fallout shelter, whatever. This works well to keep food cool and during the winter keep them from freezing too. Be careful of snakes. You can use a vent system filter to catch the air and use the cellar for a fallout shelter too.

The only other thing to do, purchase food that does not require refrigeration. Our choice is dehydrated food in number 10# cans and canned meats. The taste is surprisingly good. We have hamburger, pork, chicken, steaks and bacon, plus our veggies and lots of fruit in this manner. After you open it, place the remainder in a zip lock bag. One item you must have is lots of fruit. You will need fruit every other day or so, to keep the sugar up and the taste of it is wonderful. Freeze dried or just canned. Have lots of it.

In planning to purchase freeze dried canned foods take this tip from us. Don't purchase the one year supply all in one package with all the meals prepared for you. It was a waste of money for us. We did better with purchasing single cans of food that we used to make a meal. It tasted a lot better and we didn't spend money on stuff we would not eat, like casserole dishes.

Preserving fresh killed meat, dry or wet cures like the pioneers did can be a frustrating learning curve too. You have to learn how to dry and make jerky. There are lots of books on this and you can purchase jerky kits to help. You will need lots of Curing Salt and lots of spices to fine tune your experiments. It will take a few times to learn what to do and how much salt etc., to use for each cure job.

Now let's build a smoke house for your cures. Once again our old refrigerators came in handy for this. It only took a day and we had a nice smoke house for all our meats. To get a good tasting cure we had to travel a few miles to get Apple branches and Mesquite wood. It is very easy to make.

Just cut a hole in the top of the fridge and run 6" stove pipe from your enclosed fire box about 10 feet away, uphill to the bottom of the refrigerator. This is a cold smoke, if you want heat to cure move the box of fire under the fridge. Purchase one from the store.

Build or buy a food dehydrator for much of what you can purchase. Also build a greenhouse, whatever size you can. This really is a must for living outside the city, to be self-sufficient. Fresh things are impossible in the winter, so you will have to grow them.

Storage foods . . .

I have found out that storing any more than 500 lbs of wheat might be a waste, unless you plan to grow it. I have friends who have amassed TON'S of wheat over the years. They have nothing else, but wheat. The only way they can eat the stuff is sprout it, if they can find water, that is. You cannot move it as it is just too heavy to place on your back in a backpack. Bread is good, but there is more to food than bread every day.

Another draw-back in having a Large quantity of storage food, it might keep you from leaving your home when you should leave the area for your own safety. It might also make you a target, as your neighbors will want it, and you will want to defend yourselves, in any case you're in danger.

MY POINT:

If you live in the city, you are going to have a very hard time dealing with irate people, and gangs. The city will be in complete anarchy. Unless your block or church has an area that they can protect each other, a simple family will not survive long. If you don't have a place to run too and become self-sufficient you will not live long. That's what I think. It will be worse than anything you can imagine. It will make the "Killing Fields" in Vietnam after the war look like a cake walk. Get Out NOW!!

There will not be any stove, gas or electric, so you cannot bake bread, yet, every survival book expert I have read has told people to get wheat and lots of it. Can anyone tell me why they want you to bake bread without an oven or without the rest of the bread ingredients? You can't put it in soups or in other food ideas. If by chance you have a way to bake (wood burning oven, or Dutch oven.) the bread, you need to store all the other ingredients, honey, milk, sugar, salt and oil, etc., and you have to grind it. So, why have a lot of it. Move your thinking to Biblical Daniel's food idea, beans, rice, corn, and squashes and make soups.

At the homestead we tried to eat for two months from our food storage. Guess what we had the most of? Ya! You guessed it, wheat! I have since regrouped and started building around beans/rice for our storage. The meats and veggies are all freeze dried. That's the tip here stop amassing wheat and start getting beans/rice in its place the variety of meals that can be made are better for you and there are lots of cooking ideas using the food around you in the forest.

Plan a food that will keep the mental morale fiber up and happy. Little things mean a lot during a crisis. Charcoal, the unscented kind, and Angel Hair is used to purify water in a couple of cans by making your own water filter. Water is for your family to drink. Drink it; don't use it in the toilet or bathing.

Have duct tape and lots of plastic to cover all windows and doors if we have a bioterrorist attack. After you have closed all air from coming in your home, find a spot that you can enclose inside the home, double protection. Take the filter off the furnace and with some towels wrapped around it, you can then filter some air into the home if you need too. In this room you will need water and food to eat as well as sanitary elimination problems.

Don't forget planting seeds of all kinds. These are best purchased in vacuum packed cans or plastic sacks. The best survival foods I have found are: Barely, Berries, Cantaloupe, Kale and Beans, (black, Red and then Pinto). Don't for get the 3 sisters, Dent Corn, Beans and Squash.

Zack, Val and Sariah grew up in the mountains, off the grid. Great Kids.

Also think about moving whatever you have or have it stored somewhere where you are going to walk to, a safe area to use it, as you can't take it on your back. I will explain why later. The real reason is you will not be in your home for long during a terrorist attack or a natural disaster or anarchy; you will most likely be at work, kids at school. If we don't get a warning first we will be doing our usual daily chores, then maybe it will happen while we are asleep, who knows. We should be ready for whatever happens and when.

If you have to walk out of an area or just sit and wait for help and you don't have a lot of money to spend on storage food, think about sprouts. A five-pound sack of seeds, can keep you alive for a very long time. Soak the seeds on cloth in a canning jar and sprout as you walk or drive somewhere, it takes about 3 days to sprout before you can eat them. Each person can carry one or two jars and you rotate the eaten jar with new seeds.

If a civil anarchy problem occurs because of a natural disaster or terrorist act, or the economic crash, you will have to get out of the city and fast, if you want to survive. This has been my idea for years, and now the Government says we need to prepare to get out of the city as well, either by choice or government evacuation command. They want to move us to a concentration camp or work camp, if that is OK with you then just go along with it. If not, then you must find a place to go.

Congressmen Rosco Barlett says, "We could have events in the future where the power grid will go down and it's not, in any reasonable time, coming back up. For instance, if when the power grid went down some of our large transformers will be destroyed, damaged beyond use, we don't make any of those in this country. They're made overseas and you order one and 18 months or two years later they will deliver it. Our power grid is very vulnerable. It's very much on edge. Our military knows that.". . .

There are a number of events that could create a situation in the cities where civil unrest would be a very high probability. I think that those who can, and those who understand, need to take advantage of the opportunity when these winds of strife are not blowing to move their families out of the city. Listen to me here-you will have to leave your homes in the city to survive. How are you going to plan for leaving? You can only take a small amount of food on your back. When the plagues (flu) come you will have to leave or make an air tight and fortified home. How long can you stay in your home during a plague or disaster? This is just not practical. So, it is time to leave. You will need to hide your food supply somewhere out of the city or travel to a friend's house that lives outside the city.

If you live in a large city, such as, L.A., Las Vegas, or Boston, the harder it will be to find a place to develop a wolf trail out of danger. I don't know how to help you. Maybe you can develop a safe zone inside the city. Like a manufacturing plant, city park with a pool, large city building, something that has water, or prepares to catch rain water from the roof tops like Masada did. It must be easily protected from looters and anarchy running wild in the area. Wherever anarchy is present it will be an ugly experience to try to live through it.

Home preparedness manuals help you to plan for an emergency of a few days and then all is well, maybe the electricity or gas will go out for a while, a day or two. Get this idea out of your mind set . . . We have seen power outages from freezing rain, 1989 for instance, Canada's Hydro-Quebec power grid collapsed within 90 seconds, leaving millions without power.

If we have anarchy you will need to leave your city and as fast as possible, you can always come back, but if you are in it too long it is like the, "frog in the frying pan," it will be too late to leave, you're stuck. If you can't get out," THE GAME IS OVER." SEE YA IN THE NEXT LIFE.

In order to get out you will need a plan, *"FEMA"* has told us to get out, but didn't say how, I think you need to be more aggressive in your planning, with a way to carry equipment, kids etc with you. The old hand cart idea is a good one to use, a garden wheel barrow, bikes, whatever you can make, make it now. If you have four-wheelers great, store enough gas to get you where you need to be.

Water Well Bucket Another survival item to make is a water well, bucket. It is made from coffee cans or smaller. Cut the top and bottom out leaving one bottom. Stack two together on top of each other making a cylinder. On the can with the bottom make a small hole in the center and all the way around the outer side use a can opener to make holes, leave enough of the tin in place that you don't cut the bottom out. Find a car/bike tire inner tube rubber or something like it and cut it in a round circle to fit inside the cans, and place on the bottom, use a small bolt and large washer to hold down the rubber from the center hole.

Attach a handle on the top and a rope, cord, or wire from a telephone wire or from the pump wire that needs to be pulled out. Lower the can down the well to water. The water will push up through the inside rubber and fill the cans. When the cans are full pull the can up, the water will then weigh down the rubber and close the holes of the can. You now have water.

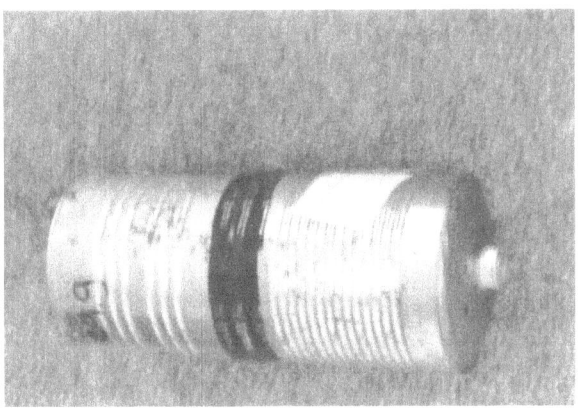

The bottom of the bucket is to allow water in and the weights to hold the water from leaking out. Inside the bucket showing the rubber lining. The first is zip lock bag and then rubber cap.

You can also make water with a plastic tarp by digging a hole in the ground to about 2 feet deep. Loosely place the plastic over the hole and place a small rock or weight in the middle of the plastic. In the hole and under the tarp place a large pan under the weight. Water will condense and drip into the pot.

Fire can be made using a Bow-drill type of tool made from a wooden broom handle or outside tool handles. Another and most likely the best fire making tool you can purchase is the "Magnesium Fire Starter"; I have used this tool ever since they have marketed the item for some 20 years. It really works well in all kinds of weather, along with this tool, if you purchase "fire sticks" you have a great combination. Beware they will only last about one year or so.

You can make your own fire sticks from Mullein stocks. Take the clean Mullein stock and light one end of it. As the fireworks it way up the stock break off the charcoal part into a large, empty saddle soap/shoe polish can and put the lid on tight to get rid of the oxygen in the can and prevent further burning of the charcoal stock. To use this charcoal; break off about ½ inch or so and place it as a spark catcher. The spark from the bow-drill will catch the charcoal and light it. Now use this long lasting spark to start your tinder. The magnesium spark will get this charcoal working very fast. Take the hot spark-charcoal and place it inside your tinder and blow. FIRE!!!

Next is the battery and steel wool idea. This works nicely if your steel wool is supper fine stuff, or your battery is big enough to set the steel wool on fire. I wrap a small chunk of the Mullein

Charcoal in the steel wool and when it gets hot enough to fire up, the charcoal is there to help hold the fire or spark long enough for me to take it to the tinder pile and fire. By using a magnifying class you can start paper on fire, or make a hot spot spark on the charcoal Mullein.

Chapter 10

Escape and Evasion

This is the way to stay alive.

We don't have the arsenal that the modern military has or the equipment to fight, so we have to use our home court advantage and get out of the city.

True life Story:
In 1995, I was in my restaurant at the Cedar City Airport when two large Army transport planes landed. The pilots came in for lunch as the passengers began to unload and to my amazement about 40 or more Russians in full military uniforms walked off. One was a two star General. They walked to a dark green bus provided by our US Army and drove off. Boy, did I have a lot of questions for the pilots. Anyway, the pilots told me that the Russians were on a sightseeing tour of Southern Utah, Arizona and Nevada. They would be looking at the land area, dams, etc., and all military post. They were here for two weeks at our invitation. WHY? I ask you!! WHY!?

We may need to run out of the city because we don't want to be there when the riots begin when Martial Law begins with foreign troops arriving.

The Cedar City Airport, about 10 years ago, upgraded their landing strips and electric radar and stuff; they can now land any airplane the military has to offer. So, why? I ask you, WHY?

A month later, three choppers landed and the crew came in for lunch. I asked the same questions as before, "What have you guys been up to . . . ?" They said they have been mapping alternative DZ's (Drop Zones) in the Salt Lake City area. WHY? He said, "For emergency drops of equipment and personnel." So, I asked why didn't they have the guys in Salt Lake do it rather than you guys from Nellis? "Don't know, I guess they didn't want them to know we were there!"

So, what in the heck is going on in this land of ours? We already know that the United States has been divided into regions and here in Southern Utah it is under UN, Russian and Argentina troops to come in if there is a problem such as anarchy. Who is in your back yard? I don't know but be sure, it is someone. Thousands of armed surveillance drones have been ordered for all the big cities by the government. So, it seems our best way to survive is to escape and evade capture. Do what we can do now while we can still do something.

It will not be long before we have Martial Law and we all have a driver's license that has an information chip in it. Next they will add a GPS and more information. Soon it will be a National ID card, that you must show when crossing any state lines or into large cities, patrolled by the National Guard. This law has already passed Congress, and is enforced by Homeland Security. Next this card will be our cashless money card or the chip. Then the government will cause some problem and the answer is to have a chip implanted under the skin, yeah, the mark of the beast is just around the corner.

You need to learn how to escape and evade and you don't have to be a military person, or have wings on your chest or have had any military training. That's great if you do, but you can learn to escape and evade without it. Be smart, or be scared, that works real well too.

SURVIVAL

S—Size up the situation, the surroundings, your physical condition and your equipment.

U—Undue haste makes a problem, don't be to eager to move; plan, think, and escape.

R—Remember where you are relative to where the enemy is and plan your escape. Where is water, where is cover, who to avoid

V—Vanquish any fear and/or panic.

I—Improvise/imagine. You can improve your situation. Learn to adapt what is available for different uses. Think outside the box.

V—Value living. Remember your goal to get out and live. Remain stubborn. Refuse to give in to problems and obstacles. This will give you the mental and physical strength to endure.

A—Act like the natives, watch their daily routines and determine when, where, and how they get their food and water.

L—Live by your wits, learn basic skills, now.

Which brings us to weapons: For survival the absolute must is a 10/22 Ruger open sites, if you have the money to purchase another one and put a nice scope on it, this is a good idea. Years ago the Eskimos hunted with a 22 for all their game food so, you can too. The open sites are best to shoot things on the run and give a better field of view of what you are looking at. The scope is for the sniper in you that hunts that way. Both are nice to have.

Another great gun to have is an over and under 22/410, this is a great hunter for small game, birds and big game if you can shoot accurately.

Then it comes to the Big gun, which can reach way out there. I like a 30/06 great power, knock down energy, then if you want to go "ma bell" you can purchase "Accelerators", which is a 55 grain bullet (22 bullet size) wrapped in thirty caliber plastic. These things have wings and can fly a very long distance. They don't have a lot of knock down energy, but that's OK. It slows down anyone following you and the best part is they can't shoot back at you, as their weapons can't reach that far. That is a great advantage when you have a shootout. Also, the rifle crack noise is so far away that you really don't know where it came from when and if you do shoot some game.

In Vietnam we were told to shoot at, and kill, but also to hit the legs and arms as this will require one or more persons to bandage and care for the injured, thus with one shot you have taken out two or more from the game. That is why the 22 is a good idea as it will cause injury and not kill.

I hope you know how to play Chess as it is a great military planning game designed to teach military tactics. If you are a hunter that actually hunts, that is walks around and tries to outsmart the deer or Elk, you have an idea what it takes to escape and evade. Do what the deer do to you every year. This is not rocket science stuff.

Plan ahead you know the ground you must go out and walk it. Stash the stuff you need to Survive. Remember to keep the other guys in sight and allow yourself as much lead time as you can before they detect you. This is the time if you have the chance to harass them with the phone idea, "reach out and touch someone" with a long shot if you like, send them running to give you time to move.

Notes for the Leader:

Water:

- Drink plenty of water! Depending on the heat, you may need to drink from ½ to 2 quarts of water per hour; that is 4 gallons or more per day in the hot dry climates.

- Drink extra water before starting any trip or hard work. Cool water (50 to 55 Degree is helpful to absorb faster than real cold water.

  - Drink small quantities frequently.
  - Drink water even if you are not thirsty.
  - Refill your canteens at every opportunity.
  - Make sure children have plenty of water.

- **If your urine is dark yellow**, you are not drinking enough water! Thirst is not a good indicator of dehydration. You need to replace your salt too.

- **To purify water** with household common bleach. Liquid chlorine laundry bleach usually has 4 to 6 percent available chlorine. For a one quart char of water, 2 drops of chlorine and 4 if it is cold or cloudy. Wait for at least 30 minutes before drinking. When chlorine or iodine is not available, boil water for 5 to 10 minutes.

- **Always bury your waste** immediately to prevent flies from spreading germs from waste to your food. Also, burying your waste helps keep unwanted animals out of your area.

- **Prevent Skin Infections;** bathe frequently, and take a full bath at least once every week. Use washcloth/wet-wipes daily to wash all parts of body.

- **Improve resistance to stress;** Fear and physical sings of symptoms of stress are normal reaction during this escape from the city. It is a life-threatening situation. You should not let fear or stress keep you from doing your job.

- Talk about it to love ones. Learn ways to relax. Give each other moral support if things are tough at times. Care for your love ones and friends. Provide everyone food, water, sleep, and shelter, and to protect against heat, cold, etc.

- **Feet;** Make sure all people inspect their socks and feet at least daily when traveling. Ensure they wash feet daily, wear clean and dry socks, use warming areas when available.

- **Medical;** One person with a fair amount of basic medical knowledge can make a hugh difference in the lives of your family or many others. Without qualified medical personnel available, it is <u>YOU</u> who must know what to do, to help others with their medical issues.

- **Dehydration:** I think the first issue to address is; **Dehydration.**

  A 5% loss results in thirst, irritability, nausea, and weakness.
  A 10% loss results in dizziness, headache, inability to walk, and tingling sensation in the limbs.
  A 15% loss results in dim vision, painful urination, swollen tongue, deafness, and numb feeling in the skin.
  A loss greater than 15% may result in Death.

- **Signs of Dehydration:**

  Dark urine with a very strong odor.
  Low urine output.

Dark, sunken eyes.

Fatigue

Emotional instability.

Loss of skin elasticity

Delayed capillary refill in fingernail beds.

Trench line down center of tongue.

Drink a little water all day long.

- **Rest:** Get plenty of rest, 6 to 8 hours every day.

- **First Aid Course:** As many people as possible.

Let me tell you a real story about a quick thinking 15 year old, my son, who saved his little brother life. They were out helping a neighbor cut down a lot of pine trees around his cabin to make a fire break. Josh was using a chainsaw and finished the cut and the tree barber-chaired back on him. The saw went up and he controlled it. He looked back at his little 11 year old bother and noticed lots of blood and Zack holding his left arm at the inside elbow. He dropped the chain saw and saw the blood squirting out of Zack's arm. His training snapped into gear, went back to the chainsaw and cut the pull rope off and used it to tie a tourniquet on Zack above the elbow. Then they walked about ½ mile home. Mother passed out and my two girls took over the rest.

We live two hours from the hospital, in Cedar City. Zack had cut his artery completely. Well, trained kids can and do save lives. <u>Knowledge is the key to survival.</u>

In any game it is not to the swift but he who thinks. Chess moves. Attack and counter attack. Make your plan to attack here when the real attack is somewhere else. Bring them into a corner. Three men teams are best. They move fast, put up dead falls/snares faster working together in sending one man away to circle and the other two set the trap. One is awake the other two sleeps. The whole idea here is to stay alive. Never attack unless you have planned an escape route. Every day above ground is a good day and you win.

- Don't spend more energy than the other guy. Got that? Never spend more energy than the other guy. You know what kind of food intake you need, conserve your energy and make him spend his.

- Don't forget the mind tricks (Rambo) to wear them down whoever is chasing you. So make sure you stay out of their reach.

New troops or foreign troops have loneliness issues that will slowly eat at them and they will get upset easily when harassed. They are also a little scared to be in an area they have never been before. Look to add to their distress by taking out the guy in front of everyone and the big brass officers. No one wants to be shot and killed in a foreign land. Think about making a trap for them, but be careful when you use an informer, I like to make my own plans and not listen to informers who might lead you into a trap. Use your own intelligence.

You can also find military field manuals that explain tactics. If you know what they are doing you can do something else. Hope we never have to use this stuff. Scares me to death, I had enough of it for real. Be prayerful, smart and don't get crazy like in Red Dawn.

Get a library of Military Trade Manuals ™ and Field Manuals (FM) from the internet or Army Navy stores.

Chapter 11

Basic Survival Axioms

Teach your family!

Fire, how to start a fire anywhere you are.

In order to start a fire you will need to have all the ingredients ready to be used. You may only have one chance to get it started due to wet weather or some other factors, do it right the first time.

Have a birds nest first of fine shredded bark, and dry as can be, this material can be a real birds nest, sage brush bark, tree bark/moss, insulation from a chair, newspaper whatever you can think of. Next is the same material but in a bigger pile. Once you have a spark burning, place larger and larger sticks on it until you have no fear of it going out and then place a larger log to burn.

Magnesium Match:

I love these. They are easy to use and it can make a fire quickly. In wet snowy conditions a supply of tire patch glue squirted onto the nest of tinder will burn for a long time and will greatly increase your chances of starting a fire with wet tinder. Scrape the magnesium side off into a nice pile, about the size of a quarter, on top of the bird nest and glue. When you strike the sparker the magnesium will go up in a cloud of smoke very fast. The glue will then ignite and you can gently blow the flame into the nest by folding the nest between your two hands and gently blow a whistle from you thumb knuckles, folding the nest when you need too. Once the fire is flaming, gently place it under your other nest and larger kindling.

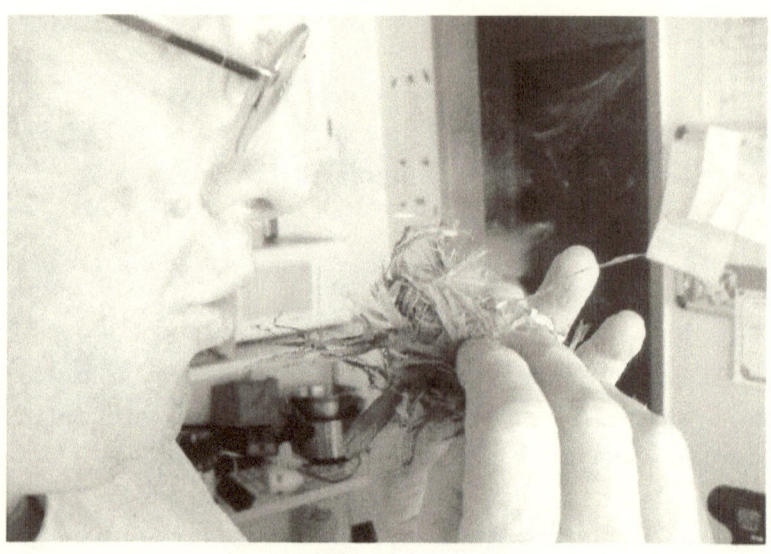

In place of a tube of glue, you can also use charcoal from an old fire or make your own mountain man fire starter by using a Mullein stock. A mullein weed grows all along the sides of dirt roads. The long stock is cut and dried unless you find one from last year. I use an empty shoe polish can to hold my fire starter charcoal. I burn the stock and break a one inch piece into the can and close the lid fast to prevent oxygen from burning the charcoal to death. When I am ready to start a fire, I use one piece of charcoal, with my Magnesium Match or Bow-Drill, to catch the spark, fold the nest around it and blow, gently.

If you are out in your car, truck, snowmobile, four-wheeler or boat and you are stuck for an overnight stay and need a fire you can use the battery to produce a spark from the top of it with two crossed wires. Gasoline can be used, but brother you don't need but a very small amount, like a teaspoon of it to get going.

Everyone has used a magnifying glass to burn ants or stuff as a kid. This is another good way to get a spark going onto charcoal or paper. I have heard of people using ice molded by warm hands to create a glass as well as glass bottles, I just don't think this can work very well, however, I have not tried it.

You can take your fire with you by using a tinder cigar shape bundle, place some coals into this tinder and then wrap it with more tinder very tight until you have something the size of your wrist and maybe 8 inches long. This will hold a fire for a few hours, about lunch time, or until you need to stop for the night.

Bow-Drill

This is really fun but will take some time to make one and learn how to use it. The drill and the bottom plate are the key to success, it must be of the same wood. You will need hard, dry wood for the drill and plate. The easiest wood to use is Yucca stem, it grows in the hot areas of desert and in front yards for decoration in places like St. George, Utah. Count your blessings if you have it available, if not I have used Cedar and sage brush. Any type of pine will NOT work at all, too soft and wet. The wood must be hard and dry. Get the knife out and lets start cutting.

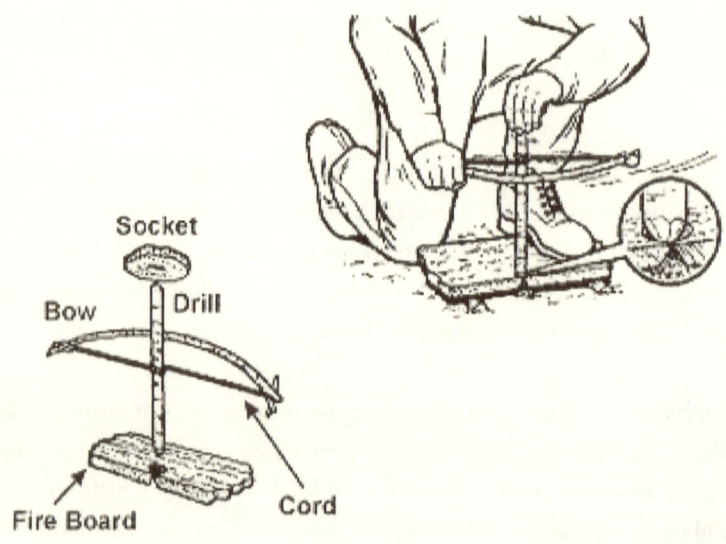

Look around where you live and find what grows there and try it out, see if it works. If not move to another tree or brush, if you can't find any wood make sure you have purchased a few metal matches for storage in cars, back packs etc.

Made from this Yucca Plant, use the stem for the drill and bottom plate. Take a look on Youtube for some demonstrations.

Other Fire:

This Mullen has many uses in the backwoods medicines and the stock is used for fire charcoal. Burn the tip and let turn black then break it off into an empty shoe polish can. The smallest spark from the bow-drill or flint will set the charcoal with a long lasting spark that can easily be placed into a bird nest made from bark. Blow gently and fold the tinder on top of the spark and you will have fire.

Using steel wool is another great way to carry a spark to tinder. Use the flint and steel or metal match to get it going. You can also use flash light batteries in a series and touch both ends to the steel wool.

Water:

You must find water to live. First lets look in the home. In your freezer, back of the toilet, maybe you were smart and filled the tub full of water when you heard of an emergency. Look at the hose outside it may have a glass or two in it. Maybe the neighbor has a swimming pool in his back yard.

You may have to dig a hole in the back yard for water to condense as I explained earlier. If you are in the Wild West, you may have to find it in the open desert or forest. First, you will look from a high spot all around to find signs of water. It may be trees, or bushes that love lots of water, willows, aspen trees etc. Maybe a canyon that looks good to you or a dry streambed that you can dig in a shaded corner.

If you find running water, great, set up camp. However, you may have to dig for it. Canyons or dry stream beds are a good place to look. If you are lucky to find a damp spot, start digging. If a dry stream bed, dig in a shady bend of the river, you will notice a lot of bushes in the area so start digging under one of these over hangs. I also look for hard rock out crops, as back in the Indian days they would carve out a hole in the rock and let the rain water fill it.

To use water effectively, you must drink it. That may sound stupid but it is true. Many dead, lost campers were found with a full canteen of water next to them. Best place to store water is in your gut. Also, don't travel in the heat of day, hole up and do what the animals do.

If you locate a nice animal trail, you may follow it and find their watering hole. However, it might be a long walk in the wrong direction. Be observent to your surroundings. My best advice is to plan ahead and place a wolf dig or at least spend some time in the area looking around with a good topo map.

How to find food?

Two types of food are available, that which you bring or that which you find. If you bring it on your back it is limited, if you have planted a wolf trail you may have enough for a while, but eventually you will have to find something to eat.

This leads us to dead falls and snares to catch rodents and maybe birds. I have produced a few pictures for you to help you understand what to do. Purchase a Bow/Arrow to hunt with. It is quiet.

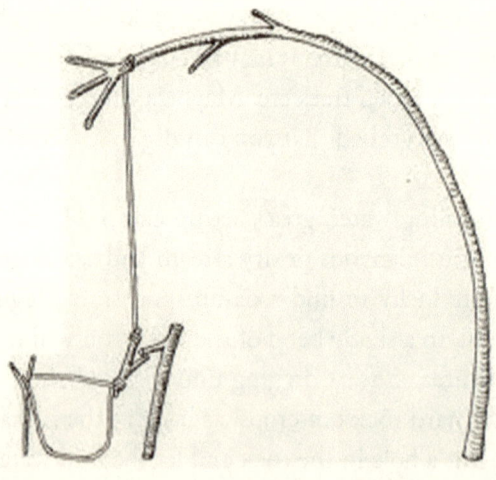

<u>Greenhouse for Sustainable Food Supply</u>

Each family should have a greenhouse in use during the year and you can make one in the wilds if you stored some plastic and rope. It does not have to be built to any great size, just use it. It will save you a lot of money on fresh food, which you would normally purchase from the store. The fact is that the grocery stores will not be open during an emergency and will probably be looted soon after the emergency. Alfalfa seed sprouts are a great food, full of energy and nutrients and a small 50 lb. sack will feed many people for a long time.

- *<u>Safety</u>*

Realize that on a national average there is about one safety officer (police) for over 400 people. These officers will be holding down their own block and protecting their own family when these events happen. It is best not to count on them for any kind of help. Here are some of the things you need to consider now:

How will you protect each other from mobs, riots and gangs? Since it will be up to you, how you do it, is up to you. Look for the weak points in your defense as well as strong points. See if your resources can be manipulated to defend against the most likely contingencies. Try to work with safety officials, if you have any you can trust. Have a chain of command that is not broken or undermined by others. Be sure you can communicate with each other. Too many ideas and nothing gets done.

If you are lucky, you may have a Veteran that can help in this planning. You always plan for an escape out of the area, too. In planning this escape plan it like everyone is the enemy on every corner.

Think about the equipment you might need to use in order to get out; night vision, dark clothes, strollers for kids, etc.

- ***Medical***

Medical supplies for; wounds, broken bones, dental problems and pain management.

Over the counter (OTC) cough drops, cold remedies and antibiotics. Little fact: Honey is a natural topical antibiotic (as if we need another reason to stock it!).

Potassium Iodide for nuclear attacks. One pill taken at the time of a blast could save your life. Get them off the web. Stop and do it now! They are very cheap to purchase. Did I mention to do it now?

Antibiotics can be purchased from the feed store and needles too. Soap and feminine hygiene products (in sufficient quantities)

Again, Do not forget nuclear fall-out, you will need potassium iodide pills. These should be available over the counter at the drug store. Somehow find how to get them in your area.

Other problems to think about; Husbands, wives and kids are in different locations all over town, miles away from home, how do they get back home to help? Kids are in "lock-down" in the school. How are you going to plan to get them out and home? What if things get so bad, that you will have to leave the neighborhood or city? Where are you going to go?

Hope you like the no fluff, straight talk.

In 1919 when the flu killed some 40 million men, women and children there was a Doctor (name unknown) who visited many of the farm country in England to see if he could help the sick and dying. One family he visited was completely healthy to his surprise. He asked the lady of the house what she did to prevent this flu from harming her family. She explained that she placed an onion in each room on a plate. The doctor took one of these onions back to his office and under the microscope he found that the onion absorbed the flu bacteria, therefore keeping the family healthy.

I heard this story from my wife's hairdresser. She said that several years ago many of her employees were coming down with this flu, remembering this story she thought she would try it. She placed several peeled and cut onions around the room and no one got sick.

Another testimony; A women had Pneumonia and a friend placed a jar with an onion in it around her bed and by morning the onion was black with Pneumonia. Many have been cured or prevented from the Black Plaque by doing the same thing.

The Biblical End

What does the future hold in my simple view?

Many people have asked me; what do you think is coming in the future? I have referred them to Isaiah and a book I recommend is "The Literary Message of Isaiah" by Avraham Gileadi. He explains the words of Isaiah in such clear and concise understanding. Another book I highly regard is the "Harbinger" by Jonathan Cahn. Both of these men are Jewish Rabbis. Please don't be prejudiced.

We here in America will be forced under Martial Law, which will be very harsh. Unlike anything we have seen in Germany, Vietnam, etc. We will have labor camps, death camps for anyone who defies the system of rule. It will be awful, beyond description of the massive evil that will be prevailed upon us by our government, Anarchy and Martial Law.

The next item to endure, we will be invaded by Russian from the East Coast and China from the West Coast. Russia will move inland and leave nothing behind but ashes. They will stop at and around Denver Co. The Rocky Mountains will be a formidable wall for them. The

Chinese will take over the West Coast. Being stopped by, the Deserts of Nevada, and in a way surrounding the State of Utah.

This is based on what I have read in Isaiah, that this war is coming from the North countries and will attack us. We get confused I think in thinking it will happen in Israel, or it can't happen to our great Country. These countries will attack when they feel that the American people are so weak from riots, confusion and our government military is worn down that we can't defend ourselves.

After that, It is up to God to deliver us and build Zion.

I have developed a newsletter that you can sign up for from my web site. You can ask questions about your particular situation and follow my updates of events. Www.familysafty.org

About the Author

- You may be asking who Dave Brown is and why should you pay attention to what he says. What type of training or experience does he have to explain survival skills in a contemporary environment? Can he tell me what I need to do to survive a riot or Martial Law? Can he tell me what to do when there is no electricity? What food storage do I need? What equipment do I need? Well give me a chance to answer you.

- I have lived it!! For the past 12 years my family and I have lived off the grid. That is the bottom line, experience. No one, and I mean, no one, can say that. You can read a lot of books out there that were written by people who have never lived what they are telling you. It is up to you, I guess, do you want to listen to someone who never had to do it or someone who actually lived it?

- I am a 100% disabled, Vietnam Veteran. I was sent to the Dominican Republic Riots with the 82nd Airborne, and saw the Watts Riots in Los Angeles while on guard duty. I have seen and been in two riots. I have seen the lawlessness of people, felt their despair and fear on the streets. It will soon be here. This is the only book out there that will tell you how to survive riots, Martial Law and economic collapse.

- This book will help you to know what foods to purchase to put your survival plan into action, going from words on paper to tangible goods that can save your life and the lives of your loved ones.

- Do you know what the Indians did for food? Do you know what the most nutritious foods for a survival are? Simply put, wheat bread, peanut butter and jam sandwichs are one of the best foodstuffs to stock pile.

- Let me show you how to buy smart, getting what you need and not what marketers and retailers want you to buy. Don't waste your money on stuff you don't need.

- I have a degree in criminal justice emphasis Homeland Security/ Terrorism and have first-hand knowledge on the subject of anarchy. I read two Jewish newspapers every day along with others to keep up with what really is happening in this world, and I believe we are in World War 3 right now.

- In Vietnam, I worked as a CIA Special Ops guy flying up and down the Ho Chi Minh trail with Air America. I have two combat jumps in that area while stationed at Udorn Thailand. I also earned my Thai (Thailand Army) jump wings.

- I medically retired from the Army in 1969, and it wasn't long before I had to get away from city life and I ended up in a little town called Hamilton, Montana. I lived there from 1973 to 1979. It was there that I opened a survival school under the name of Pioneer Survival School. I was also an outfitter and guide for bow and black powder hunters. I trained with Smoky Elser of Missoula, where I learned to (Decker) pack horse for the trail. I've taken people/kids into the mountains of Montana for a week or two with nothing but a pocket knife and a blanket.

- We found 20 acres of land in Southern Utah and built our home there. I have learned a lot about living off the land for the past 12 years and even more about what NOT to do. This is not a book of some fat, old, bald headed guy writing from his living room comfort. My family and I have lived it, experienced it and fought Mother Nature for this homestead. Let me tell you how we did it and how you can prepare for an a natural disaster, terrorist attack or how to just be self-sufficient.

- Other credits have been: I was on ABC 20/20 with John Stoussel as a paralegal suing the Utah State Bar for not allowing the poor and indigent access to the legal system. An article appeared in the U.S News and World Report on my business of providing do-it-yourself legal forms to the public.

I pray it never has to, but this book can help save your life